# VANGUARD OF NATURE

BOOK ONE

OF THE SERIES

NATURE AGAINST HUMANITY

T. WILLIAM PLEASANT

# VANGUARD OF NATURE

BOOK ONE

OF THE SERIES

NATURE AGAINST HUMANITY

# VANGUARD OF NATURE

Cover design: Michele Leite, Lisbon, Portugal
Formatting: Enchanted Ink Publishing

ISBN: 978-1-7365598-3-3

Printed in the United States of America

T. William Pleasant
P. O. Box 8876
Missoula, Montana 59807-8876
USA
Website: https://twilliampleasant.pubsitepro.com

To Dr. Marina Kanyevskaya,
who would get all the inside jokes.

# Author's Note

This text contains scenes of physical violence, combat, sexual
violation, and thinly-veiled obscenities

In dealing with Nature as a *de facto* character, human nature
shows its face in ways both beautiful and ugly. This is never
meant as an endorsement, but simply as an attempt to
honestly portray the characters in an authentic light.

# CONTENTS

*". . . But for good people to do evil things, that takes religion."*

—STEVEN WEINBERG, DINOSAUR

# Prologue

*St. James Park, across from 192$^{nd}$ Street Intersection...*

*...At the dawn of a new day, and of our New Natural History.*

*T*he call of an automobile's horn overshadows the soft, soothing rumble of the 4 Train in the distance, an aluminum millipede moving south on the elevated tracks. A band of Norway rats, about a dozen or so, forage through a trash bin by a park bench, ready to follow their tribe's unique pheromone back to their subterranean hovels. House mice crawl in between copies of the New York Daily News— yesterday's news, yesteryear's news for what it's worth—smeared with milk curdles and gooey, dark brown tomato sauce. The five-day-old coffee grounds smothering a photo of Mayor La Guardia dated in Dinosaur Years 1936 don't have such an inviting aroma as they would have a few nights before. One of the mice finds a clump of dried oatmeal, encrusted with sugar and soured milk. She takes the delicious morsel to the top of the trash piled in the bin. Her left foot rests on dinner, a french fry, just deep-fried yesterday. Up in the trees, gray squirrels with white fluffy tails that never stop flicking back and forth make their way to the center of the park. Beyond them stand the gates and fences that keeps humans out *for now. As all three species mill around, getting their nourishment from what they can find, they all gather without mingling, sniffing the concrete. The gear-shift sound of a diesel truck joins the truck's exhaust fumes that blend with the putrefying offal stink from a distant dairy farm, filling the neighborhood with their unique stenches, providing a sharp contrast to the aromas of the budding trees, and the patches of grass pushing upward, feeling for the coming sunshine. The sun hasn't risen. Yet, the park has that gray, dim-light shadow where vision is no longer impaired. All the rodents go their way, minding their business. Then suddenly, each perks up, sniffing the air, listening intently through the terrain's silence, standing upright, frozen in awareness. Though each is myopic, seeing only in focus to the end of their tail, in their diminutive brain the size of a walnut each still sees something . . . a slate-gray rectangular monolith . . .*

## Chapter One

# IN HIS ELEMENT

I t has been eight nights since we of the All Rodents Evolutionary Union (AREU) attacked humanity in this great natural change, the next Great Extinction. Our Great Sacred War for Evolution will save our watery Earth from her planetary death caused by humanity. According to the wisdom of our Glorious Big Cheese, Comrade Steely, within one hundred nights our beloved Earth will be free from humanity in all three of its genders: male, female, and feline. That leaves us ninety-one nights after this one to fulfill our glorious evolutionary victory. Every rat in the All Rodents Evolutionary Union knows humanity can't be beat in only one hundred nights, but nobody has the iron greasy grimy gopher guts and unshakeable courage to squeak a thing. Even I, the usually out-squeaked Fearless Litzkachew, executive commander of both the Rocky Mountain and Wabash Fronts, have to keep my muzzle shut. But even with my blend of cerebral power and feisty fury body, my restraint won't last forever. Despite the courage, reproducibility, and resilience of the Rodents Liberation Army, our brave RLA, we can't just throw one hundred nights into the kitty and expect the enemy to drop dead. The fighting forces of our Union will need to invest time—our most valuable commodity—into the effort. Even so, as each night we fight for salvation, humanity strives for full planetary extinction.

Both fronts I oversee champ at the bit to liberate the southern Rockies, across those political entities they call Colorado, Utah, and western Nebraska. Together, under my command, they compose the Rocky Mountain Strategic Direction. The Rocky Mountain Front, in the Colorado Rockies, extends north into Wyoming, and south to La Trinidad. The Wabash Front covers the mountains east of the habitat known as Salt Lake City, and points north to Boise, Idaho. Over two hundred million well-trained rats, house mice, flying squirrels and other species serve our Union as fighters in the Rodents Liberation Army. The over a half a million fighters of the Rodents Liberation Army Air Power (RLAAP) and sea rats of the Rodents Liberation Army Navy (RLAN) in North America will join the RLA to take part in this greatest event in natural history. Add to that the half a billion militia rodents in their workers' and gardeners' uniforms, who fight in their spare time between tending their gardens and manufacturing the implements of Rodents' War. Tonight, all hurl themselves against an enemy that took for granted that they—humanity—went to the moon and back with Dinosaurian technology. The humans bear the potential to do so much good, yet they choose to be destroyer, instead of savior.

On the outskirts of Denver, out of the night sky my staff and I drop down to land my flying command post next to a Su-Sto (Cy-100) copy that we call a "su-sto"—a turret-less tank with a .30–06 barrel sticking out of the hull. To us rodents, "helicopter" is a Dinosaur word. We call any rotary–winged aircraft a cheebah. Our cheebah's fuselage, painted in gray camouflage patterns, bears the one-word meme of our Rodentian superorganism: "Evolve!" Stenciled in black and white under the portholes of the door at my right, this idea drives our taxonomic order to save this greatest of planets in the cosmos through our evolution into becoming the prime animal. "Evolve!" Painted on the fuselages of our warbirds, the turrets of our tanks, the black banners of our count-less regiments, the RNA/DNA in our genes, this word has the power to drive us from our primitive past to become the prime species of the animal kingdom, the vanguard of nature, the standard-bearer species of evolution, the true paragon of animals.

The brigade executive officer, or ExO, sits outside of his own su-sto next to the one I'll ride into battle. I jump out of my cheebah, scamper over the snow, then leap onto my tank to the open hatch.

"Jump!" I squeal.

"For?" comes a response from the dark interior.

"Joy!"

"Get in! Please, Comrade Fearless."

I hop down the hatch as if it were a gopher hole. The tank commander, Senior Mechanical Specialist Grumpy Fishbone, turns on a light that illuminates the interior, with its light gray walls and its smell of axle grease and gun-cleaning oil. The tank vibrates from its engines as I find my place in the interior. I move my tail to avoid what just might be the most common injury in the Rodents Liberation Army's Armored Corps: crushed ratty parts.

The unit rumbles past the sewage treatment plant on Emperor Drive between Lafayette and the burning Louisville. About eighteen clicks away, liberated Boulder sports our black flags and banners flying from flagpoles and windows; liberated in less than a week! The unit drives down the road toward State Highway 42, to hold the junction of 42 and Highway 287. We make it to a bridge, where we take incoming mortar and small arms fire.

"Give me the mic!" I command.

"Yes, comrade!" calls the radio operator, who also serves as the hull machine gunner. I take the headset.

"Buggy Bumpers, this is Command Post Dozen," I squeal with authority. "Buggy Bumpers to Command Post Dozen! Acknowledge!"

"What do you want?" comes the rude reply. As I get ready to fire a salvo back at that ExO, he replies gingerly, "Excuse me, comrade!"

"Herringbone at the tree line! Take those farmhouses!" I command.

"Affirmative!"

Like a metal turtle shell of a bell, our su-sto rings with the impact of an enemy rifle bullet hitting its side.

I push a lever on the headset with my muzzle. "Command Post Dozen! Command Post Dozen! This is Slinky Mink!" I call over our intercom. "Everybody! Off the road! Herringbone! Herringbone!"

"You heard the rat!" commands my tank commander. "Do it!"

His order gets our tank to shift over to the right. Our su-sto builds speed, then throws us forward in our battle stations as we stop abruptly. At the intersecting off-road position, where we all take defensive positions—evens to the left, odds to the right—we all wait for the ExO's voice.

"Dismount!" he orders the fighters. They're all running on adrenaline and intuition at this time. Then, more units with sixty or more armored vehicles roll up through the fields behind trees by an icy stream. Motorized infantry and armored grenadiers pop out of their armored fighting vehicles and try to advance across the frozen stream. Enemy fighters of the Colorado National Guard and human irregulars in goose-hunting gear set up a hasty defensive perimeter along the other side of the creek. The black smoke from one of our technicals burning at the entry of the bridge drifts back on our RLA fighters. We started this fight for evolution with hundreds of chopped-down Dinosaur cars and trucks, remanufactured with armor- and crew-served weaponry. Those are our technicals. And we're losing them as fast as we can build them.

"Gunner, identify . . . Three forms through the trees . . . Eleven o'clock."

"Identified! Full metal jacket! Five rounds on the ready! And three soft-nosed!"

The calls back and forth between gunner and loading crew stops when the su-sto stops.

"Perfect!" squeals the gunner. "Down range!"

A loud beep almost bursts everyone's eardrums. Then the action of the main gun punches back with a violent thrust.

"Nice!" exclaims the tank commander. "Direct hit!"

"Siblings! I saw that pig jerk up into the air!" comes a joyful comment over the intercom.

One of our armored vehicles takes a hit just on the other side of the stream. We know this type of eight-wheeled

armored personnel carrier as a Bump 80. "Vehicle down!"
comes the squawk across the intercom. I sniff the air, listening intently, trying to sense what's outside. Around us, more
armored fighting vehicles are emptied of RLA motor infantry
and armored grenadier units that leap through the snow like
a herd of well-armed and tiny deer. Something hammers our
tank, jerking us backward. Then we stop.

"Gunner! Identify! Shadowy forms in the bushes to the
left!" The gun moves to the left, pulling the breech over to the
right. Then the breech bounces around.

"Down range!" calls the gunner. A loud beep in the ears.
And the breech bounces back with a violent jerk, then returns
to its resting place. The action opens, the bolt projects back,
ejecting a smoky empty shell casing that rattles on the floor.
Then the loaders use a tiny crane to drop another round into
its magazine.

I call over the intercom, "Tank Commander! Comrade
Fearless! I'm de-tanking!"

"Yes, comrade! Thanks for letting us know!" comes the
reply.

I pull myself out of the open hatch. With bare paws on
the cold iron, I leap into the snow, then head in the direction
of the enemy. I clothe myself with chaos, with complete focus
on the moment, finally in my element. The winterscape is cold
and all, but I don't care. Projectiles, like quick-flying hornets,
buzz directionlessly around me. They hit hard surfaces, then
whine after they ricochet. I feel so alive, so close to death! I
scamper past the now blazing eight-wheeled vehicle, with its
burning tires offering a filthy smoke screen above the clean,
fresh snow. I sniff in the direction of its open hatch, smelling
the last three survivors as they hop out—the last one on fire.
Burning Last Rat lands in the snow, runs a short distance, then

rolls around in a tall snowdrift. I hop onto the frozen creek's surface. One of our antihuman gun teams trains its fire on the nebulous human forms crawling toward us from the base of a tree. Another RLA team fires a machine gun on a two-wheeled carriage. The guns go silent, so we all listen intently. Across the dark gray snow, the yappy sound of RLA cavalry drifts over to the streambed, as three thousand partisans on dogback charge into the enemy. Boston terriers and beagles trumpet a bawling war cry of their own, leading the cavalry forward with a sound more effective than their bugle calls.

The smell of burning cordite trails a burning fuse as it drops on the machine gun. All the fighters put their ears to the air and noses toward the last noise. A bright flash accompanying a thunderous shock wave erupts on the fighters, ripping them to smoking pieces. Incoming rounds spray dirt and snow in my face. The loud shrieks of our stricken fighters pierce the cold air. I sniff the air in their direction. The shrieks continue. I hop over to them. Finding one comrade, I take the wounded fighter in my jaws and pull the brother backward across the ice toward the liberated side of the stream. The ice explodes all around us when a Dinosaur round hits nearby. Two other brothers join us. Then a sister scampers right into our impromptu crew. I draw a sigh of relief when I see a medical satchel from one of the corps' female brigades of combat medics on her back. All four of us get the wounded rat up the bank, where others take him out of the battle zone.

"Any others?" asks the sister.

"Yeah. Follow me," I command.

The sister and I scamper back toward the other wounded. Sniffing the air, listening to the surroundings, we try to get to the others by following and focusing on their screams. Out beyond the streambed, by a tree in a gray pasture, an RLA tank burns as a Bump 80 races to its side. The vehicle stops, as a load of fighters leaps to the snow. Then the Bump jerks, issuing a cloud of smoke. The report from a 12.7 mm sporting rifle follows the impact. The fighting vehicle burns as fighters scurry out of it, chirping for direction and commands. Enemy fire blows gray geysers of snow in the air, showering the brave fighters as screams come from their direction.

"Can you hear them?" I ask.

"Out there. Can you see that big tree?" she replies.

"Hardly." With an uncorrectable vision of about 20/300+, I see only blurry forms in that direction. So I use my other senses. I scurry in the direction of the screaming, which blends with the whimpering of the wounded in the streambed. I stand up, to connect with our wounded fighter brother. "That's him! Follow me, sister."

The girl rat complies, and we scamper to the burning tank and vehicle by the tree. More incoming Dinosaur rounds buzz past, some bouncing off the snow past our ears. Other tanks and APCs charge toward the farmhouse beyond. We reach the carnage, and sniff around for survivors. The brave sister finds one, pulls out a Band-Aid and bandages the whimpering wounded. I rip off a strip of fabric from the rat's battle dress, then bandage the wound on a scorched crew rat from the burning tank. A round grazes his backside, then ricochets off the tank. I pull the wounded to the lee of the tank, then join the sister. We tug the Band-Aided fellow back to the lee, then a round rips off the sister's medic satchel.

"Sister! Hide under the tank!" I command.

"No!" The good sister grabs the wounded again and helps me pull him until the wounded rat is out of sight of the enemy. I stand behind the tank and sniff the polluted mountain air, detecting burning fighter flesh, rat blood, dead Dinosaur flesh, and a farm building behind where the shooting originates. And the whimpering of more wounded. I follow the sad cries to another and grab him with my jaws. Another round hits the brother, but I get him back to the hiding place. I sniff out the wounded rat's body, then I feel the brother die in my paws. The sister pulls another one in, burned and ripped up. The tank takes a round, shaking it violently again.

We two rescuers sniff and cut open the uniform of the wounded to get at the wound.

"Brother . . . I want to die. Save yourselves," hisses the dying fighter, no more than four months old.

"Comrade," peeps the sister, "Let me hold you, then." She gives him a rat cuddle. "Thank you for your sacrifice, brother." She piles up snow onto his burns while I grab another. I pull in another young one that has his right eye shot out.

"He's going to make it. Let's get a Band-Aid on that eye," I chirp to my partner.

"Let me smell," she replies, sniffing the wounded fellow's eye. Out comes the last Band-Aid, and over the empty eye socket it goes.

Once bandaged, we take the wounded in our jaws, then drag them through the snow past the streambed to the liberated piece of streamside ground where my su-sto sits. The farmhouse with the gray metal roof burns in the distance. Bullets rip the snow around us and the wounded, but we have a goal. Save these siblings. Because this is what we rodents do. Our personal interests mean nothing. Collectively, we are all one.

Once on the other side of the stream, the wounded fighters disappear into a large white ambulance converted from a liberated Dinosaur van. The brave girl rat scurries over to that other farmhouse where both a temporary command post and first-aid station have been set up.

"Shee! Sister!" I whistle to the fearless retriever worth more than her weight in gold. She doesn't answer, just keeps on scurrying, out of my smell range and vision, and out of my life.

## Chapter Two

# WHO IS THAT GIRL RAT?

I'm not looking for another sex buddy. My special someone, Catnip, shares all of that and more with me. Yet on some other level, that unknown or unnamed sister has captured my soul. Her complete lack of fear, or complete embodiment of courage . . . something like that, I don't know which, touched me because she embodies what I love about us rodents. That girl rat is a microcosm of our taxonomic order, Rodentia, mother to us all.

It's been fifteen nights since Night One. We've completely liberated Boulder, and in our paws we hold sections of this town, known as Denver in the Dinosaurian tongue. The airport still resists. Hundreds of humans scurry through miles of tunnels underneath it—their own concrete burrows. They must have learned it from us.

A temporary thaw warms this liberated haven within Denver, which is still mostly infested with humans. At the intersection of York Street and 9th Avenue, a chipper and fine-smelling prairie dog comrade stands with directional flags in her paws. Of all the females in nature, the most nubile Rodentia are the prairie dog girls. She holds her arms close to her uniform, flipping the black-and-white flags to direct an oncoming convoy of RLA trucks that rolls past her, moving to their destination at the nearby Botanic Gardens. A Big Cheese 2 tank, carrying a dozen or so of our mud-smeared but cheery fighters rolls past her. On its turret, written in white Ratsqueak letters trimmed in black, is the slogan, "All for Rodentia!"

"What are you doing after the war, my little chickadee?" asks one of the fighters, with two of our disposable antihuman rocket launchers strapped to his back.

"I'm going to be the mayor of my town," she whistles back.

Along comes our su-sto, battle-scarred but purring like a happy kitten. From the bustle rack in the back, our black banner of the Union flies proudly in the breeze with its silver fringe flapping. I hang out from the side hatch, steadying myself on the roof as I gnaw on the machine gun.

"Sister! Can you direct us to the temporary record-keeping center?" I whistle at the prairie dog.

"I can't even see who you are! I won't tell you anything!" she shrieks back.

I know this is war, so I can appreciate the fact that the female fighter can't let a loose whistle betray our army to our enemies, so I thank her in response. "Thank you for your silence!" I call back to her.

"Move it!" she replies with a bellicose whistle. Heroic female fighter. These girls will bear our victory on their shoulders, I think to myself.

The su-sto finds its way to the new command post of the Rocky Mountain Front in a liberated multi-story condominium, with most of the Dinosaurian human stuff left behind for us to sort through and make nests in. I roll up maps and battle plans and stuff them into tubes before we scurry into the basement. The situation room of this impromptu command and control center was a laundry room until we removed the washing machines and put huge maps of Colorado and the Rocky Mountains all around. The building next door houses the transitional hospital that Catnip just moved to. She saves lives and bandages those physically shattered in the nearby field hospitals when ordered to, but at least she'll be close to her beau rat.

Hanging on the outside of the northwest corner of the condominium are squirrels garbed in blue laborers' uniforms with army web gear strapped around their bodies. They wrestle with a new public service announcement device that both broadcasts from the central information network and listens in on our conversations. With two big black bionic ears sticking out of the dome-shaped guts, the Inner Union can identify anyone who suffers from "soul sickness," that personal condition of being one's own sovereign self. The squirrel brothers plug in the device. Behind it, as though it were watching all we do, a portrait of the Big Cheese rolls down, secured with paste by a laboring chipmunk. Under the black-and-white stylized visage of Steely, the statement "The Big Cheese Hears All!" reminds us that we are never alone. The device comes alive with the whiney voice of a porcupine reading a list of commodities as she announces the glorious victory with the success of the First Three-Month Plan.

I scurry into the new command post with a cardboard tube in my mouth. Pack rats pull in boxes of scrap papers. Our regional archives rest comfortably back in the Central Command and Control Center under some mountain overlooking Boulder. But who pops into this operation? None other than the Rocky Mountain Front's archivist, Comrade Executive Director Eech Shishishkurchakee, that aging pack rat from liberated Boulder.

"Have the Rock Mountain Front records been set up?" I squeak with authority, being the alpha rat in the Rocky Mountain region.

The executive pack rat stands up on his hind legs and sniffs, "Who's asking?"

"Comrade Executive Commander Fearless Litzkachew, executive commander of the Rocky Mountain Front!" I throw at him.

"Never heard of 'im!" whistles a laboring woodchuck in that characteristic Marmotian accent.

"Shut up, Charles!" shrieks the executive pack rat. "State your purpose," chirps the aging pack rat at me.

"You mean you don't know who I am? I'm your chief union boss of the Rocky Mountain region!" I chirp back in anger.

"That don't mean diddly cat scat!" the pack rat counters. "How do I know you aren't a spy?" That's the first time I hear that bogey bunny—what the humans call a "boogeyman."

"Sniff my marking pheromone," I command.

He sniffs the air around me, wiggles his whiskers, and then lifts his fury pack rat tail. "Comrade, if you're the regional leader, then what brings you here to the movable archives?"

"I met a female rat in combat about a week ago, when we liberated some Dinosaurian 'burg. Lafayette, the Dinosaurs called it. I have no idea who she is, and I'd like to find her so I can bring her onto my staff." I use my whole soul to get a feel of his response.

"What does this girl rat do?" asks the pack rat.

"She's a golden retriever. Haven't heard that term before?"

My jargon from the battlefield leaves this rear echelon bug-thorner stumped. Then he wiggles his whiskers with suspicion at me. "And why is she so important?"

I feel contempt for this aged keeper of our history. "Because the best baby-batter and breeders will be forged in the fulcrum of combat. Something you may not understand," I reply.

"So in other words, you just want to give her the ol' thorn!" hisses the pack rat who hasn't seen combat.

"I want her on my officer staff as an apprentice," I respond.

"I bet you do," chirps this ancient archivist, bleeding out his own contempt for me in his aura. He sniffs me out again and doesn't find me to smell familiar. "Comrade Fearless, I am not authorized to disclose information to the brave members of the Rodents Liberation Army."

"And so your regional commander is untrustworthy?" I inquire, my heart losing its qi.

"Only the Big Cheese himself can earn my trust. I may immediately respond to his request. And he whistles, 'No.'"

Over the two big ears of the listening and squeaking device, an annoying squeal torments the ears of us all, sounding like slate being scratched. Then comes an announcement straight from Universal City. "Attention, attention! Your attention please! The Voice of the Species has an absolutely mandatory announcement! The supreme director of the All Rodents Extraordinary Committee, Comrade Commissar Pike Dzinkfish, announces evidence of a conspiracy within the Inner Union to remove our courageous leader, Comrade GenSec Steely, the Big Cheese himself, from his rightful position as leader of the Union. More details will follow as this affront to our security shows itself! Squat by for further developments, siblings!"

The pack rat heard every word! He pops into a fighting posture, muzzle aimed right at me, and challenges me with, "And why should I trust that you are who you squeak you are, comrade?"

The building shakes from a direct hit. I scamper to my tank crew. "Back to the su-sto!" I whistle with an alpha's authority. Other rodents stand up, their souls grasping for a sense of what's happening.

At the tank, I follow the last crew rat in. Then I pop out the hatch on its roof. Our tank farts out a huge stinky cloud of diesel smoke. I sniff out the machine gun, then grab the handles with the trigger button in between. I swivel the weapon around, pointing the barrel in the air.

I may command the two fronts in the Rockies, but I don't command the tank. As the crew inside the tank chatters at each other over the intercom, the tank commander, or T.C., pops out the commander's hatch next to me.

"Wheel right!" orders the commander over his throat microphone. I aim the weapon down the street as our tank rolls east under the bright manifold-shades-of-gray cloud cover. The antennas on the vehicle sway with the movement, with the black flag of the Union flying proudly at the top of the tallest one, and a liberated triangular flag of the Mickey Mouse Club under it.

"I thought we had this area secure!" I squeal to the T.C.

A bullet explodes on the front of the tank. Metal shavings rip into my muzzle, but I feel no pain. Just everything else in the ratty soulscape. I fire the machine gun at what appear to be moving forms. My vision isn't the strongest, so I really don't know what I'm shooting at. The T.C. drops down into the tank, then our riding lawn mower–size battle wagon fires its main gun. Ahead of us, three humans (I think) in the battle dress and equipment of special operations forces pull a wounded comrade behind a burned subcompact. I point the machine gun at them, as the tank faces those enemy fighters with its main gun. Together, we target those two-legged Dinosaurs, those reptilians.

"Eat death, you shaved monkeys without a tail or hope!" I shriek as my curse-squeak drowns, washed away with the rattle of my weapon. The main gun outshouts us all with a word, punching out a Dinosaur. The beast hits the snow and sidewalk, bleeding out its lifeblood, its carcass to be refrigerated for the cooking crews that will turn it into stew. The other Dinosaurs drop dead on the snow, joining the first. The su-sto rolls up the snow-carpeted concrete walkway to the steps leading into the pockmarked condominium across the street from the new command center.

I scurry out of the hatch, then onto the hot metal of the tank's rear. The hot metal balances out all the cold of the winter snow and ice. Attached to the bustle rack on the back, a brace of three disposable antihuman rockets hangs. I chew off the duct tape securing the rockets to the rack, then throw them over my shoulder. The T.C. pops out of the commander's hatch again.

"I'm going inside, brother," I hiss to the rat in charge.

"Driver! Turn the tank around 180 degrees! Yes, Comrade Fearless! We'll guard the entrance!"

I leap into the crusty snow as the tank turns around, barely missing the treads that could grind off my tail. Scampering up the walkway, a whole lishek moves toward the su-sto, about

forty of our fighters in all. They are not unlike sperm cells
meeting an ovum, with their ratty tails swaying behind them.
Each has a black bandana around his neck, and the black arm-
band of my Central Command and Control Center staff constabulary on their left foreleg. Rodentia's finest. In the street,
other rodent fighting vehicles roll past.

I scamper through the entrance, without backup. Being
alone could make me look like a deserter. But I'm still in charge
of this Rocky Mountain Strategic Direction. So, I do what I
please. The door to the staircase stands agape, beckoning me,
daring me to scurry up its steps into the unknown. Challenge
accepted!

Hiding in these ruins, humans still hold out, waiting for
their government or something else to rescue them. Or just
for that skeletal ferret the Grim Weasel to come down and
eat them. The Grim Weasel is our Grim Reaper, so maybe she
doesn't bother with humans. But I will defy that skunk and live
for eternity out of shear spite if I ever find out that the Weasel
is the lapdog of the Reaper.

Anyway, I sniff around in the ruins, crawling upstairs to
another floor. I come to the landing of a hallway. I scamper
down its long emptiness, sniffing the air, smelling what wreaks
of a fresh and dirty Dinosaur diaper. I follow the stink, then
hear the low vibration of a baby's scream, followed by the
faint rumbling voice of what could only be a female human.
From the spirit of the female, I sense she is the mother. I
creep into an apartment through a door that's slightly ajar,
giving me comfortable room to walk in on all fours. I follow
the wall for a ways. The place has been kept clean by the enemy. We've never been here before. I can tell this by the lack
of rat or mouse pheromone. I freeze when I make out the
occupants of a leisure chair. Gently rocking back and forth

now, a dark-skinned human sings a song to a bundle in her arms. I can't tell if the baby is still alive, but I can hear the mother weeping as she sings. I sniff around some more. The other rats scurry throughout the first floor, but I'm the only rat up here. I pull out one of the human-killing rockets, shoulder it, ready to fulfill my duty as an animal meant to exterminate all humans. But a wave of etheric energy flows over me as I smell the helplessness of this doomed Madonna and Child. The protocol is to kill all humans not on the exclusions list. I would guess 99 percent would never make that list, especially the displaced ones like these two. To not follow through with that protocol is evidence of cowardice and weakness. Softness is weakness, the greatest threat to Nature. But in this moment, I refuse.

I relish the kill, though it's never really the kill itself for me, but the thrill of the chase. Nonetheless, I shoulder my weapon, hoping this Dinosaur finds her way to a postwar life, making her peace with her Grand Mother Nature. She still doesn't sense my presence. I back away, turn around, then bump into the wall. Out in the hallway again, I scurry back down the staircase, and out of the apartment. After we make our way back to our vehicles, I will fill out my official report with the statement including, "No live enemy engaged in the ruins."

## Chapter Three

# NINTH ALL RODENTS INTERNATIONAL

I n North America, two rat species make our presence known. We so-called roof rats name ourselves in our own language the Shriedaygahbayan, Shries for short, Shriedaygahba in the singular. Like myself, that special someone Catnip, who will litter our pups, and hundreds of millions of our fellows who make their homes in attics and treetops, we Shries fight to earn respect and recognition from the other rodents. Inclusion fights like a cornered rat against that problem hidden in plain sight, *speciesism*.

The dominant rat species, the one that ranges across this continent and dwells in subterranean places, is the Dzumban. In the plural form, it's Dzumbani, or what the Dinosaurs in North America call Norway rats. Norwegian makes a strange adjective in any language. Dzumbani condescend us Shries, calling us "tree dwellers," "squirrels without bushy tails," and "disease carriers." And we fight over resources against them as they force us out of the better habitats and the best food and water sources. The few of we Shries who became general secretaries of the AREU in its 462-month history have been prevented from exercising real power. The Dzumbani who support Shries (and there are many, believe me) are themselves treated terribly by their own kind.

In the history of our taxonomic order, we rodents probably killed each other more than the humans killed us. No cat ever called me a Jeemsh. That slur against my species comes from my Rodentian siblings. I am a Shrie, not a Jeemsh. My species' name comes from our words meaning glory. I squat as a free rat. To call myself Jeemsh would enslave my thinking.

Six months before I meet Mystery Girl Rat in the midst of cold winter combat, the warmth of the summer solstice embraces the Ninth All Rodents International convening in an abandoned warehouse. With filthy water from the roof dripping down into buckets among the delegates and service representatives, we conduct the business of our Union in the midst of what I, as a clean rat, consider squalor.

Yet the assembly of the Ninth International draws over four thousand participants. Dressed in the efficient, simple yet well-kept uniforms of each branch of the armed services, the labor force, and the political services, the rodents sport shades of green, blue, gray, and natural cotton colors. Absent from the color scheme are red, since the rodent eye lacks that retinal receptor, and black, since that would be too negative.

As Chairmouse Fearless, I squat at the chair's commanding position in front of the assembly. (Whoever squats at the chair position, whether boy or girl, no matter which species they identify as, is referred to as the chairmouse. Tradition.)

The whole assembly attentively listens to my dear friend and mentor, that scorpion mouse of renown, political philosopher from the High Desert, Supreme Doctrinarian of the Union Eech Sheep Poker. Over eighty months ageless, Comrade Eech does mousy martial arts with a dojo full of kangaroo rats for an hour every evening before breakfast, and he can still make short work of a Dinosaur-killing scorpion. Doctrinarian Sheep Poker uses a dry piece of linguini to poke at his diagram, which hangs on the clipboard that dwarfs him.

"The thesis/antithesis dichotomy adds the negation of the negation, thus giving us the dialectic of thesis, its negation antithesis, and synthesis, that negation of the negation which brings the two adversaries together to mutually edify each other in a higher reality of truth. This is our meeting place as we scamper along the path of ultimate peace and prosperity in Nature's happy destiny.

"This mental construct, originated by the house mouse philosopher Eepsheep Pepper Jack more than thirty months ago, structures our meme as our backbone structures our bodies. Now, we hold it in our souls as the foundation of our dogma. Our meme. It states that Nature functions by the paradigm of thesis, the primary meme. The meme of the protagonist. Thesis is the protagonist, my dear siblings. Antithesis, which negates the thesis, is the protagonist in its own hero's journey. Synthesis, which negates the negation, brings protagonist and antagonist together in harmony by resolving the conflict between the two when it takes each of the two conflicting agonists to a higher truth. This is how Nature functions. Grand Mother Nature operates within a paradigm, a pattern that can be clearly defined. Basically, Nature is a superorganism in its own right, constructed from so many smaller superorganisms. And our superorganism, the All Rodents Evolutionary Union, is no different." The mouse puts the pasta to the side, then looks the whole assembly in the beady eye.

"Siblings! Comrades! Our Union-wide foundation is one of a shared responsibility for the functions of our service structure. If personalities overcome this principle, we will become enslaved to that personality. No one personality represents this Union any more than any one rodent represents our species. Therefore, I recommend we always hold to that principle that provides an equitable means of reconciliation and unity among the siblings. Let us always squat and gnaw our chew sticks in synthesis!" The assembly rewards him with a hearty applause.

Scurrying down the sewer pipe after the assembly breaks up for the day, the doctrinarian and I sniff each other out, recognize one another, and wiggle our whiskers in siblinghood. My brother smells of a powerful confidence and conviction in his personal doctrines. And I can see Sheep Poker does life without a right ear. One left ear and one ear left, trademark of the supreme doctrinarian, former general services archivist, and bad-tailed scorpion-killing desert mouse.

"Comrade Chairmouse! I have a gift for you. Right from the archives of the Supreme General Service Office," squeaks my fierce spirited mousy mentor.

I thank him in advance with a fearless sniff his way. "It's nice to know I won't go home empty-pawed."

Shortly afterward, we squat together before a veiled, flat object towering over us.

"Brother?" Eech addresses me in that familiar salutation, "Logistically squeaking, what's the most important commodity we can produce?"

I wiggle my whiskers at the doctrinarian, "Knowledge! That goes without saying."

"But what about information?" asks the mouse, who then gnaws on the discarded leg of an old wooden chair.

This takes me by surprise. "Information is the ore we mine from the data dumps of humanity, then process with our superior intellectual souls," I respond, weighing my words, not entirely trusting the doctrinarian at this point.

The mouse puts the chewed wood to the side, thoughtfully rubs his belly with his paws, and then gazes at me with those brown mouse eyes. "You're an educated rat."

"Self-educated more than educated," I add, qualifying the statement.

"But you can grasp this thought . . . He who controls the past controls the future . . ."

". . . And he who controls the present controls the past! That's the motto of the General Services Office Archives!" I chirp.

"Exactly!" whistles the mouse. "The new general secretary could be a dust brush. Sweeping away all the previous knowledge. What if she or he creates an alternative history?"

"We could have an alternative future!"

Then the scorpion mouse throws out, "And if that future makes us so de-rodentized that we become . . . humanized?"

"We could be the next extinct species, like the humans are now. Almost, at least." I reciprocate. Then I sniff out the chair's leg for a dry section.

"We could damn ourselves to become the next humanity," he adds, then gives the wood a chew.

Afterward, the doctrinarian unveils the gift, revealing a portrait of thirty-five rodents squatting together around a college blue book liberated from some Dinosaur student. Underneath each of those rodents of renown, the writing systems of several rodent languages appear in white, identifying each

by name and office. Underneath the white lettering, in that ancient form of Ratsqueak, is the script, "All Rodents Evolutionary Union. Let us Begin in the Here and Now."
I cluck out a sigh of amazement. "Dinosaur year 1977. Thirteen nights after the summer solstice. The original Foundation of the Union Day."
"This is an original and should never be replaced," adds the mouse. "Guard this connection like our grandmother's very life depends on it!"

The election for the new general secretary ends with a tally on the chalkboard to my left, house right, as run by the executive elections committee. Our associate chairlady, Senior Advisor to the GenSec Office Brie Grainbelt, a girl house mouse from some small city in the Rockies, stands at the podium in front of me. To my right, directly behind her sits our supreme doctrinarian. I gnaw on the desk.

At this moment, Brie presides as the official tally-er, reading the results into a microphone as a porcupine wielding a piece of chalk writes on the board. ShBri announces the news from the elections committee concerning the appointment of the new general secretary.

"We have an official vote count. Of the 3,993 delegates qualified and eligible to cast their votes in this election, we have . . . first off, fourteen duplicate votes and thirteen ineligible votes, all of which will be discarded. Of the remaining 3,980 votes cast, 468 count as abstained. The minor candidates—all twenty-seven of them—garnered a grand total of 1,308 of the votes. We will publish the election results in the *New Rodent Illustrated*, so you can go there to get those figures. From the five major candidates, from the least to the most: Dzumban Cheerful Mustard Seed garnered 162 votes; my fellow house mouse Aromatic Cheese Cloth brought in 210; our well-known representative of the Wind River Prairie Dogs Gutsy Thorn Bird brought in 398; Sage Bunting, our European representative of the Shriedaygahbayan, all the way from her warm hovel in Limerick on the Island of the Shamrocks, goes home with a vote of 538; and finally, with the rest of the count at 886, our new general secretary as of the fall equinox, three months away, brother general service representative for the Rodents' Republic of Dzo' dzya, in the municipality of Marietta, the home of our burgeoning rocket and missile industry—"

"Just squeak it out who won!" comes a voice from the assembly.

The strong-willed and ever-intelligent house mouse in charge commands, "Silence! I have the floor now! Brother Dzo Dzugash Veeley, our very own Comrade Steely! On behalf of the whole Supreme General Service Office, and the All Rodents Evolutionary Union, big congratulations from the executive elections committee!"

The assembly gives an enthusiastic applause to the future helmsrat of the Union, as Steely stands up to accept the praise, and get a smell of those who aren't so enthusiastic. Beside him, his associate, Brother Pike, the tall, lanky Dzumban from Chee Kha Go, scribbles names and lack of enthusiasm into a notebook.

"She didn't have to use my whole name," Steely whispers to Pike. Pike writes that down as well.

"Squeak, squeak, squeak, squeak . . . !" The auditorium that has full buckets and crankcase oil from another decade on its floors fills with the demand for a squeak from their new union boss. With pained expression on his muzzle, Steely tries to put on a gracious air. He glances back to Pike.

"I have a bad feeling about this."

"Don't let it show, brother. This is our chance," replies Pike, whispering in Steely's small Dzumban ear. Being a good showrat and actor, Steely manages it well, as he scurries to the podium. Steely masks any insecurity with his affable public servant's face, accompanied by an almost jovial disposition. Relaxed, confident, comfortably in charge, Steely stands to accept an even warmer, more hopeful applause.

"Siblings!" Still more applause. "I really wasn't prepared for this, but I appreciate your trust and faith in me." The audience gives him more of what he craves. "Siblings, you can all rest assured that your Brother Steely will fulfill his duties. Without a missed note." More applause. "I know I can be worthy of it." After a shrill standing and excited ovation, Steely continues, on the surface appreciative, but annoyed underneath. "Our order, the order of Rodentia, calls us to unity, service, and natural recovery . . ."

The speech is a hit. The natural charisma of Steely intoxicates the service members of the Union, making them giddy with their decision.


The future Big Cheese began his journey through the corridors of power as a little first-born Dzumban. Brought up at the northern edge of the Dinosaurs' urban sprawl the humans call Atlanta, Steely grew out of his given name very quickly. Yet that name invokes a foreboding caveat. Dzo Dzugash Veeley, as he came into this life, took that name from his great-grandfather, who personally skinned sixteen feral cats. Steely grew feisty in a rat family where his dipsomaniac of a father lived on stale beer, that liquid bread, and wouldn't share anything with the pups nor their mother but violent anger. Dzo means "first" in the Dzumban tongue, so it was fitting that such a marvel of service should be christened with a name meaning such. He and all his litter siblings took names ending in the "o" sound. Young Dzo answered to the name One Peep, given to him by his mother, Hope Brilliant Sunrise Dzugash Veeley. Months later he would take the name Steely, after he picked up a ball bearing in his jaws. It takes a rat that's stronger than the ball bearing to be able to lift such a metallic sphere. The name stuck, and he never would dream of rubbing it off.

Steely moved around a lot in those nights. The litter went with their mother to new spaces between walls, in garages, compost heaps, woodsheds, and underground burrows near landfills, to escape the violent, drunken outbursts of Steely's father, Sheekh Dzugash Veeley. As the first born of his siblings, Steely watched over the rest, bearing a burden of responsibility he cherished. Sheekh spent his nights eating whatever the family could bring home from foraging. Then he would go out to find half-full cans of beer, and the last ounce or so of wine in Dinosaur bottles marked T-bird. Like all rodents good or bad, Sheekh stole anything and everything that wasn't too heavy or too much work to take. As the night sky lightened above, the father repeatedly came home to bully the mother for sex and bite the pups for no reason. Steely learned early to defend his mother and siblings. After three months of abuse, Steely helped the family disappear from scent, moving into the spaces of cinder blocks in the foundation of a huge laundry service facility. There, Steely put his newfound love of learning to practice as he read sales receipts, then magazines in the eating area where the siblings gathered food out of the garbage, teaching himself to read the Dinosaur Squeak they call English. Thus bitterness took a back seat to the pleasure of the text. Steely grew in cerebral prowess and power, with his will forged into a resilience worthy of his beloved name.

Steely took advantage of an opportunity to get a formal education from a school run by Rabbitarians, those rodents who worship the divine masculine and feminine in the image of Mother Rabbit and her son, the Big Bunny. Steely became a bright student and a brighter troublemaker—the kind of pupil that can either become a smashing success or a slippery criminal. Steely loved history and social studies, and on the football field he excelled as the captain of the team. Teams from the various academies and schools played football, or *kuli sneezlee*, as we squeak in our lingua franca, Standard Ratsqueak, with Ping Pong balls stolen from the Dinosaurs. Every rat loves to steal. It's in our blood. Our DNA. And Steely the Stealer was a thief extraordinaire. And a schoolyard scrapper!

Everyone respected his exceedingly strong will, the power of his intellect, his passion for life and his family. Yet no one remembers ever actually feeling love from the diminutive dynamo. If anything, Steely had spirit like no other, but no soul. And his eyes were a tomcat's eyes. Cold, predatory, always sizing up his fellows. Always sniffing out potential enemies. Always harnessing his fear, to channel it into action, to advance his position. If Steely learned anything from his father, it was trust no one. And Steely was an apt student.


"Perhaps the Sacred War within our own souls must be won before we take on the Dinosaurs," I ponder out loud to the supreme doctrinarian, as the scorpion mouse and I share some pre-meeting fellowship. At the final general assembly meeting of the Ninth International, the two of us stand at the podium of the assembly hall, enjoying the fellowship of thousands of siblings, all gathered in harmony. No speciesism, no hierarchy, no prejudice at this second.

Who should come up behind us, preceded by the stink of his bullying spirit? None other than the incumbent general secretary, scurrying ahead of his entourage. He brings his bad cheddar-smelling attitude with him right into our proxemics zone, doing what he can to break our concentration. To devalue my position in the Union pecking order, the pesky trusted servant whispers into my ear with a whistle.

"Jeemsh." Steely hisses out that ethnic slur against us Shries. Right in my big Shrie ear! So I place the microphone away from my muzzle and up to his, where the future Big Cheese can't see it. "Who thorned your Jeemshy mother . . . Turn that damned thing off!" Reverberating across the hall, the assembly squats in stunned silence. I pull the microphone away and put it in front of my own muzzle.

"Go home, Dad! You're drunk!" I teasingly command.

The shock turns to a cacophony of high-pitched shrieking mirth, as rodents across the assembly grab their bellies in laughter. An enemy of the species is created.

At the end of the election night at the Ninth All Rodents International, I stand before the assembly at the podium, that pulpit of love that draws all good rodents back to Grand Mother Nature. For it will take love of Nature and one's species to go forth from this International and cleanse the polluted and adulterated Earth. At this second, banished from the assembly is the mirth of the tête-à -tête between the next general secretary and me.

I saddle myself with the great burden resting on our shoulders, as I smell the variety of species meeting in this convocation that constitutes our Union. With a humbling joy, I take the microphone stand in paw, and gnaw on it as the Great All Rodents Choir of the Siblings finishes that magnificent hymn, "All of Nature's Glory is a Halo for Our Union." Afterward, one of the gerbils blows the bugle call, "First Assembly." All in the meeting squat upright in unison as we sing the rallying anthem of our armed forces, the RLA's official song, "We Serve the All Rodents Evolutionary Union:"

*Onward, to the glorious victory*
*Serving Nature's life and liberty*
*We stare down death and dishonor*
*And put fear and treason on the funeral pyre*
*We will swim a mighty river*
*Sail the nine seas*
*Fly through fiery iron AAA*
*Together, we proclaim our allegiance with our true battle cry*
*"We serve the All Rodents Evolutionary Union!"*

I dominate the floor now. The Ninth All Rodents International assembly passes into the books with this final address. Behind me a banner proclaims, "Humanity can no longer claim to be evolution's primate! Rodentia answers the call of Nature with low-tech hardware and evolutionary spirit!"

I sniff the microphone, bite it, and then pee. "Brothers. Sisters. Siblings in the family of animals," I begin. "We all carry within ourselves the call of Nature that leads us to this most pivotal moment in natural history. From here, we will fulfill with confidence the will of victory! The great oversoul thinks the sanity. Emotes the divine passions. Acts out by the power of the natural will, led by Her divine wisdom. Thus the new, fair age of the order of Rodentia will be built upon the burned rubble and ashes of the ending world of humanity. Nature goes forth from this assembly, the Angel in the Whirlwind stirring the cleansing fires that shall consume all of humanity's indiscretions and iniquities. Evolution is the force of Nature driving destiny. Our destiny. Where once humanity stood as the supreme, the primate of the animal realm leading evolution's imperative, it now lies fallen. Fallen. Ready to be replaced by you and me. From this moment forward, we are the new vanguard of Nature! Let no beast stand in our way!"

## Chapter Four

# THE CALL OF NATURE

Rodentia celebrates Nature's New Year with merriment and homemade cider on the evening of the winter solstice, December 21st. I perk up my Shriedaygahbah ears to the announcement over the PA system, with its tinny sound emitting from the squeakers, as we call them—squeakers in every corner. The Big Cheese reads the proclamation of war preparation over the international public address network, with his shrill squeak punctuating every consonant of his heavy Dzo' dzyan accent, spoken in Standard Ratsqueak.

*"Siblings! Comrades! Let us therefore gird the loins of our souls and answer Nature's call together! Let's lift our legs together to victory!"*

A thousand meters underneath Poison Ridge in northwest Colorado, the Central Command and Control Center, the headquarters of the Rocky Mountain Front, mines its way through the rock like a luna moth's caterpillar cocooned in granite, hidden in plain smell amid the machinery and open spaces of Production Plant Complex Rhe-Chee-Chee #9.

We siblings of the northern Rockies Front Central Commissariat stand on our hind legs, with rapt attention on the metallic voice coming through the squeaker, a lingam/yoni symbol of our capstone of leadership, as though Shiva and Shakti are met in the pronouncement. The Dinosaur-made horn squeaker, liberated by a team of evolutionary thieves that procure for our cause, rattles a little with each twang of our GenSec's accent. Ruling the space over the squeaker is a poster-size portrait of the Big Cheese with a crowd of rodents behind him, all dressed in the work and battle dress of our industrial workers and gardeners, fighters, sea rats, and flying squirrels. The Great Rat thoughtfully gazes beyond the viewer to the brilliant future, as he sits up on the foundation of Rodentian power, a book. Knowledge is power. The greatest asset we can mine.

I recently assumed the duties of the secretary of logistics, quartermaster general of the All Rodents Evolutionary Union, but I still retain the honorific Chairmouse. Behind me, dominating the subterranean space is a table covered with maps and little figures of rodents and cats: us versus them. Regarding we rodents—the Chosen Children of Nature—our two genders blend in beautiful harmony. The Dinosaurian humans, with their gender confusion, fight over this question: Who is the supreme gender: masculine, feminine, or feline? The plastic rodent figures represent our armies within the Rocky Mountains. Looming behind the table above all the officers and other ranks, the portrait of the Original Thirty-Five looks down from the concrete wall where it securely hangs, the long-deceased founders observing the Central Command and

Control Center staff as they give all attention to the voice of the Big Cheese.

*"We hate the Dinosaurs with a righteous rancor!"*

I sniff around. My ears perk up, scanning the smell- and soundscape of the room. Everyone else is mesmerized by the proclamation. Then I push this group psychopathy aside for a minute and gnaw on a chew stick made from a fir twig.

*"Brothers and Sisters. It is my greatest pleasure and privilege to lead all two billion of you in our righteous cause. Without all of you, your comrade Steely would be no one."*

"Forward, comrades! Siblings! Into the twilight we scamper!" the gathering explodes.

A mouse-sized pup of a fighter scurries up. "Chairmouse Fearless, this is the greatest night in natural history! And you're making a racket with that chew stick." I throw the chew stick by a well-chewed pebble on the concrete floor.

"Brother," I opine to the angry little mousy RLA recruit, "If we inherit this earth like we're supposed to, it will be because of all of us together. As equals!"

"But we are all together. With the Big Cheese. Are you sure you're with us, comrade?"

This cheeky dishonor from a youth for one of the most experienced trusted servants will not go unpunished. "Fighter," I hiss as I bristle, trying not to interrupt the webcast, "Get back to your post."

"Don't confuse your rank with my authority," responds the fighter.

A meter away, three Dzumbani show up, sniffing the air around me as their whiskers vibrate. Their tense whispered squeaking betrays the religious extremism they call dedication. Others tense up around them, reacting to their perceived air of authority. The solstice proclamation of our Great Sacred War for Evolution against humanity concludes with a rousing rendition of "We Serve the All Rodents Evolutionary Union." I, along with the young fighter and all the others in the room, join in. All except the three serious Dzumbani of the All Rodents Extraordinary Committee.

As night approaches—the ultimate darkness of the longest night of the year—stands a deserted, dilapidated mansion in the Hamptons. Windswept and sea sprayed, it's a house that at one time would have been right out of Fitzgerald's *The Great Gatsby*. Inside, a poster-size copy of the portrait of the Original Thirty-Five appears on a wall, with Steely, newly named the Big Cheese, superimposed in front of the other rats. As though he were there. A large group of rats gathers in the main dance hall. In a prominent spot under the portrait, the Big Cheese, wearing a stiff-collared white jacket sporting metals and trimmed in grayish gold, stands up on a brick in the middle of the group, towering over the others. Because he's smaller than the other rats. On a raised platform by the large fireplace, chipmunks in a musical band play fast-paced dance music.

All the others gather around half-gallon jugs of vodka that are tipped over to pour their contents into crystal trays that the rats drink from. They are dressed in formal military attire and stiff-necked coats like that worn by their leader.

"The crystal is from Berdine's," the Big Cheese points out. Two hours ago, Steely wrapped up the reading of his war proclamation, which all good citizens of the AREU have just heard. Now he grabs everyone's attention. "Anyone up for a joke or two?" The rats crowd around Steely in thinly veiled nervous anticipation.

"Oh, yes. Yes! But of course!" squeals the audience.

The Big Cheese continues, "Why did the chicken cross the road?"

The audience acts stumped. "Uh, uh? Let's think."

Executive Commander Hissy Cat Hairball, a Dzumban larger than most, stands to make his point.

"Truly, your logic outshines our capacity, Comrade Steely."

"Obviously," replies Steely, getting to his point. "To get to the other side." Steely chuckles, as though it were an original thought. The rest join in with a forced good-natured laugh. Steely continues. "Why did the turkey cross the road?" He looks at Brother Anthrax, a medium size Shrie with noticeably big ears characteristic of our species. "Well, Brother Anthrax?" The good comrade feigns deep thought.

"Uh . . . to get to the other side?"

The Big Cheese gives the ol' beady stink eye. "Wrong!" squeals Steely to the whole group. Brother Anthrax cringes, his eyes widen in fearful anticipation. "To prove he wasn't a chicken." The crowd is dumbstruck. What brilliance! Then they crack up in feigned hysterics.

"Now. For the most important and salient point." Everybody else crowds around the Big Cheese. "Why did the drunken human Dinosaur cross the road?" The crowd draws a blank. "To get to the other gutter!" The crowd explodes with forced laughter. The disappearances of those who don't appreciate such humor have already begun. "Pour that purloined Stolichnaya stuff! Let's drink!"

The music resumes. The bottles come down, filling more crystal from Berdine's. Whoever she is.

Catnip fell in love with me the first time she smelled my aroma.
And I fell for her spirit and her good health. A prime littering
machine. That's what we guy rats say when we get alone with
each other. Tonight, Catnip stands behind a surgical table created from a piece of two-by-four covered with a lint-free blue
towel. She is practicing the triage of likely survival candidates.
Within eleven nights, these skills will be used for saving our
fellow rodents on this upcoming journey. The greatest evolutionary event in natural history, natural present, natural destiny.

Zoologists teach the educated rodents that great shifts
come upon the Earth, wiping out whole life-forms, then re-
places them with more capable ones. The superorganism of
Rodentia prepares itself for this event. Now, thanks to the
wisdom and leadership of the new GenSec, the call goes forth,
so the Union makes final preparations. Catnip counts liberated
Band-Aids and daydreams about me, her smoky good-smelling
special someone. And soon, we will be grooming each other
on the Natural New Year.

The seconds pass like weeks as she sniffs each empty nest
waiting to be filled by the glorious wounded. In her thoughts
she arches her tail up for her rat, vibrating her ears, enjoying
my ratty part. And from her muzzle, passionate chirps of ecstasy provide a soundtrack for her pleasure as she feels my
celebration of her girl rattiness. Every lusty squeak from my
muzzle is her soul's comfort. She saves this for me, and me
only. A one-rat girl rat.

Another nurse scurries up to Catnip. Just like her, this
nurse sports the new loose-fitting white scrubs with the blue-
and-white epaulets of a senior nurse. The senior nurse sniffs
out my girl, but not like I would.

"Senior Nurse Catnip Litzkachew!" the new nurse addresses Catnip. My girl rat stands at attention, with her paws

hanging down, her muzzle turned up slightly. "Third shift's taking over, sister. Anything we need to know?"

"I have the bandages put together in the nine boxes out front, and the cheesecloth sits in the drawer with the no-lint blue towels. I was just finishing all this bedding."

"I'll take it from here. Thanks for everything tonight."

The two stand together, bear their incisors in the salute of the RLA, and in unison repeat the time-honored statement, "We serve the Evolutionary Union!"

Out of the hospital, Catnip scampers home to her rat. The hormones gush through her arteries from that pre-lovemaking scamper. The greatest aphrodisiac for her is that heady cocktail of love and exercise.

Catnip always longs for her beau rat when I'm not with her. She would never want one that's less than best-of-breed. And she wants no one else but me. She sees me as a prime example of the New Natural Rodent, that standard of excellence representing what a nubile girl rat wants her beau rat to be. Honest. True to his core values. Kind and considerate on the outside, unstoppable and ferocious on the inside. Gentle to his fellows, unmerciful to the antinatural enemies of our taxonomic order, Rodentia. Dynamic. A rat that answers that call to a purpose higher than himself. A builder of our world. Always in motion, always active, not unbalanced in the cerebral nor the physical, but scurries within that happy medium between the two, bringing the left hemisphere of his brain together with the right, so that the two work together, blending well, complementing each other, just as the masculine and feminine are meant to.

Thus far, Catnip aggressively approves of her choice. If we were Dinosaurs and not humanity's superiors, we would have unearned tattoos all over our furless bodies, pierced nipples (both of 'em!), and metal things sticking through holes in our noses. She would wear those black spectacles that were popular in the last century. I would quit listening to my former favorite band, the Bunny Worshippers, when they become too mainstream. We would shop local, grow our own vegetables, eat ethically produced grasshoppers, or just be vegan. We would think we're asexual after having tried to be hypersexual. And PBR wouldn't be a patrol boat on a river, but the hipper-than-thou cheap cat pee in a can with a dead comrade mouse at the bottom.

I want to retire to a big tree overlooking an old Dinosaurian hovel, where Catnip and I could live like squirrels and raise up a couple of litters. We two love-bugs would smell a big co-operative garden out back, which every member of the co-op works in, and from which we all would get our own grass-hoppers and brussels sprouts. And a warm, cozy root cellar would be underneath, somewhere, where we could grow fresh veggies and raise bugs for the stew pot during the cold winter moons. And a creek would run alongside it, contributing its water to the hydroelectric plant we would build ourselves to power our technology. Together, several rodent species would live in harmony, teaching their pups that we are all beautiful as we are, and so are all the others as well.


Clothed in battle dress, the kangaroo rats thrust their subma-chine guns forward as they hop righteously to the other end of the stage. In unity, they sweetly sing the "Song of the Species" from the Grand Evolutionary Ballet's production of *Triumph of the Species*. Directed by Madam Snaketooth, the Most Cre-ative Girl Rat Ever (her official title), *Triumph of the Species* takes the stage as the latest and most meaningful example of evolutionary performance art. This magnum opus stands as an important accomplishment, destined to be enjoyed by trillions throughout all-time. With its depth of emotion, and amazing visual appearance, it proclaims the hero's journey of the Big Cheese's rise from an Atlanta slum, to becoming the standard bearer and elder statesrat to the species, the order, kingdom, the whole Earth, even to the ends of the perceived cosmos. Such an inspiring and powerful story! And in it every rodent who experiences it, no matter what language they squeak, can understand the suffering and exaltation of such a life, the life of the Big Cheese. Larger than life! The lifts he wears in his footwear notwithstanding, the Big Cheese stands on the gigantic shoulders of kingdom animalia with perfect balance. And no one loves him like his female consort, Snaketooth. Helpmate to his greatest self, she squats as his concubine, better half, nest mate, advisor, and confidant. Mother of his pups (three sons who have survived to adulthood, and a daughter, Girlgoat). In a holy marriage ordained by Nature, the wondrous passion of love bonds the two in a beautiful, mutual dependency, naturally drawn together as the prime example of the roles of the male and female. As the goddess/god androgyny of Nature divides herself rightly in two, becoming one flesh, so do Comrade Steely and his divinely creative partner Snaketooth love one another.

"We are masters of our own hovels! We are rulers of our own fields! We are owners of our own machinery!" The songs of Nature's freedom from the oppressive Dinosaurian age ring out in an eloquent squeak from the All Rodents Evolutionary Choir. The lyrics land so naturally on the animal soul.

As the curtain falls on the second act, the heroic girl rat character Comrade Senior Fighter Kali Catskinner whistles to the audience, "Let the Dinosaurs fight with Dinosaurian tactics! We fight on a nonlinear battlefield. Tonight, Planet Earth is the battlefield. With the blood of the martyrs, the whole Earth with be sanctified, cleansed, reborn!"

Cultural evolution is at work cleansing the soul of the species and order, preparing Earth for a new night. Snaketooth pushes it to get her own slice of the power pie.

Later, after bouquets and roses celebrate the end of the production, the two evolutionary lovebirds meet in the throne room of power.

"Where's my little chocolate cupcake?" Steely purrs to his beloved Madam Snaketooth, who washes herself in a liberated sink now used as a bathtub. The aroma of green apple shampoo blends with the smoke from a censer, where incense made from rose oil turns the bathroom into a temple of sensual worship. Over the small and quiet loudsqueakers, slow, soothing sounds blend with the comforting babble of a mountain stream.

"Is that my alley cat?" replies the madam, getting clean and fresh for her beloved.

"'Myeeook, myeeook,' says your tomcat."

"My very own tomcat of evolution?"

"The one and the same, you best-smelling girl rat in all of Nature. Right there with my mother," replies Steely.

"Up here in the warm waters of your affection, my love," she calls with an intoxicating chirp. At that request from his special someone, his partner, Steely the Great Rat and Great Leader of Evolution's Destiny, scampers to the sink, following the path along the wall left by the rats in this domain. He jumps up to the walkway to the sink, then crawls into the waters, uniform and all. Snaketooth smells him to make sure it's really him, then pisses on him, marking her territory. Her urine blends with the soapy water to give a unique aroma of holy union between the two.

"How do you feel about your ballet?" asks Steely, as he grooms Snaketooth in the water and urine.

"*Triumph of the Species* is going to be the greatest thing ever in my life! It's what I've worked my tail off for all my fifty-three months," she coos. Steely nuzzles her with loving affirmation.

"I know. That's really why it means so much to me."

"And it's your hero's journey," she shares.

"And your passion," he reciprocates.

Snaketooth snuggles up to him even closer. "And you've been the greatest support a girl rat could ever ask Nature for."

"And I'm your greatest admirer." The two nuzzle, groom, and then do it on top of the faucet, with that shared affection of the truly bonded by the goddess. Together they will listen to forbidden music that smacks of the taste of a Wild Turkey whiskey sour slush ("Love and Passion" from Cheryl Barnes!), knowing their bond is stronger now than ever before.

Meanwhile, after the night has been put to nest, I bond with my beloved.

"There you are, tomcat," calls my beloved and oh, so delicious Catnip, sniffing my tail hole. "Mm, love that musky aroma!" she squeaks.

I get my muzzle up to her lady rat parts and lick that gateway to the mysteries. She pulls her tail into the air for me, a rat cobra pose, and wiggles those big Shrie ears. So I sniff her vibrating ears, tickling her face with my wiggly whiskers, and then I walk my paws down her back until I enter her in our divine union of the masculine and feminine energies. "The greatest twenty-one seconds of my life," purrs out of her muzzle.

## Chapter Five

# NIGHT ONE, YEAR ZERO

S alt Lake City sits quietly under a partly cloudy sky, the smell of the Doug fir trees on nearby mountains blend with the exhaust of automobiles and the bodies of two hundred thousand humans, not counting those of their feline third gender. The clouds in the skies above reflect the glow of the city's lights below, joining its nighttime brilliance, choking out the ease and comfort of rest with light pollution. The Year Zero is eight minutes old. A new age in natural history begins. The skies above the mountains northwest of the city center fill up with warbirds of the RLAAP. Like vultures in the bright desert sky, our rodent-built raptors circle in a holding pattern waiting for the incoming warheads to immolate either Toole Army Depot or Hill Air Force Base. From the airstrip, a flight of four F-16s takes to the air, while a half dozen other metal warbirds get ready to join them. Across the continent, our special attack task forces crawl into the inner workings of the Dinosaurs' aircraft, chewing up the wiring and hydraulics of those multimillion-dollar warbirds so vulnerable when perched.

Above the sleepy mountain city, the final stage of a missile fired from that launched brace of six arcs down toward South Salt Lake, away from the Salty Sea. The payload stage discards the last rocket motor with three blasts from the primer cord wrapped under the top stage. Then three banana peel doors open to fall away in the slipstream, exposing the warhead, a propane tank from a gas grill, now filled with sixty-nine explosive lenses aimed at each other, each with weapons-grade plutonium smeared over them. They demand to go critical with the sixty-eight others. The plutonium-filled propane tank attached to a recycled D-something-plex business computer drops toward that large Salt Lake City suburb. The compartment underneath it opens, deploying a paraglider. The device slows down to a comfortable speed, directed to its erroneously perceived target. It thinks the cloverleaf intersection below is its intended target, Hill Air Force Base, when it floats into position above Interstate Highway 15. Still a good shot, but not like it was supposed to hit.

A flash that blocks out all vision temporarily drowns the night in an ocean of glaring light. Our subterranean fighters waiting for the bugle call crouch, sheltered from the lethal flash. Then a deafening "Bam!" The flash dims, giving way to humanity's darkest fear, a brilliant and fiery pillar rising to the heavens, hoisting a cloud of smoke and nuclear terror. From the epicenter above the cloverleaf of the Veteran's Memorial Highway and the Belt Route, ten or so clicks from the intended target, an orange and black mushroom cloud rises, proud of the soul damage and trauma under its power. As that slate-gray cloud drifts eastward, it reflects a flash from another strike above Rose Park, just east of the big airport we hope to utilize.

Six clicks above El Paso there exists a crossroads of two cultures, each claiming the city's soul. The glare of the city streets directs the flight of six four-engine warbirds onto their intended target.

"All warbirds! Shade the interior!" commands Brother Senior Air Officer Peepee Cricket. The crew members comply. A flying squirrel with the heart of a Dinosaur child sits on his desk in formaldehyde. Air Officer Cricket pulls the shades closed in the cockpit, then pulls a glass lens made for welding masks over his eyes.

"Bomb away!" comes the squawky transmission from the intercom. As the warbird levitates from the loss of weight, the screechy squawk over the bomber's intercom becomes as comforting as the gentle chirping of the pilot's own pups.

"Fifteen hundred meters," calls the bombardier in charge of the ordnance delivery.

"Brace yourselves," commands Cricket.

If Fort Bliss burns under a mushroom cloud, the RLA will devour the remains of the city unopposed. Soft targets will destroy themselves against our guns and rockets.

Officer Cricket's warbird jerks up violently, then Cricket bounces into the stale, oxygen-poor but latex smelling–rich air of the cockpit. His bushy flying squirrel tail spins in fear as his eyes widen behind that blackened lens. The whole crew swoons. Then the bird quiets down.

The crew returns to the tasks at hand, pulling the shades open, and safely looking out the canopy glass with beady, naked, myopic eyes. They observe the brilliant rise of a mushroom cloud, flames, and shock waves plowing over the suburban landscape underneath. The cataclysmic cloud stands over the stricken city, the rod of correction against humanity's seat of learning. Like the glow from a comforting campfire, the pillar of fire illumines the fog of the shock waves shrouding the city. Then it burns out, leaving fire across the debris as the only light from below. The senior air officer gazes in a trance, filled with the thrill and joy of a successful task. He focuses on the controls of the demanding and argumentative warbird, levitating inside from the power in his accomplishment.

"Rooster Sauce! Rooster Sauce! This is Tarkio Two."

Cricket answers the call of his wing squirrel. "Go ahead, Two."

"The gadget pulled off a full yield! Five kilotons!"

"Affirmative, Two."

Cricket remembers his fellows. "Tarkio Flock . . . this is Rooster Sauce. Thank you all for your hard work." Several of the other birds key their microphones in agreement. And Cricket admires the flames below, knowing he has now become Death, Destroyer of Worlds

Fifty-nine minutes into Night One, Senior Medical Retriever Cappuccino counts the Band-Aids in her combat medical pouch. Crushed against her, the medical retrieval crew she commands, thirteen in all, waits for the whistle to go forward up the crowded tunnel out into snow-blanketed Boulder, Colorado. The shriek of the alarm causes all to fidget with hostility. The tunnel vibrates with the shock wave from an explosion at the end of the tunnel. Our gopher engineers scamper to the newly created entrance.

For the next half hour, they clear the exit of debris. A bugle call whistles through the tunnel. Rats garbed in white smocks scamper past Cappuccino and her crew. Cappuccino sniffs at the last fighters of a special reconnaissance unit as they scurry past.

"Crew Thirteen! Gas masks on! Get your gas masks on!" Cappuccino commands her charges. She scratches her cream-colored fur, then dons her gray rubber gas mask. Her crew slowly trudges the long, dust-filled path and scurry to the edge of the tunnel. Where the lights end, all direction must now come from the sensation in their paws. The tunnel envelopes the retrieval crew with darkness. As they grope their way to the entry, they feel the winter chill. The crew mingles with a lost gopher of the engineers, then they are against the concrete edge of a sidewalk. Cappuccino's muffled squeak hardly penetrates her gas mask. She pulls up the standard-issue penlight she lugs around, using its forbidden light to rally her crew. They all come together. After identifying each one, she ties a piece of kite string from her pouch to each of her retrievers. All accounted for, Cappuccino ventures out into the dark gray and navy-blue night with her crew, with only the sound of snow falling to accompany them.


The beauty and horror of nuclear clouds rising to assault the heavens shakes humanity's soul throughout the Dinosaur habitats of Europe. Under a partly cloudy and chilly sky, London awakens to the flash of a two-kiloton blast over the Bank of England building, its epicenter being the Cornhill-Threadneedle-Cheapside intersection in the southeast. The blast immolates the bank shatters that funky blimp-shaped geodesic edifice to the east called the Gherkin, as well as its skyscraper neighbors. Yet St. Paul's stands resolute. And London Bridge is standing up, strong with a stiff upper lip. The first air raid over the city since 1945 is met with the whiney rumble of Tornado warbirds as they head out to intercept our RLAAP.

Paris, Brussels, and Rome suffer the same fate. Yet none of the weapons used accomplishes a full yield, any more than in London. Paris shakes under its attack as southeastern suburbs burn, yet the landmarks of the city still stand without inflicted trauma. NATO Headquarters in Brussels takes a direct hit, losing its surface buildings for show, but not its officer staff, nor subterranean command post. The papal offices on the lawn in Vatican City take an unholy blow from the strike intended to vaporize the world's smallest empire. Yet Saint Peter's Basilica refuses to crumble. Aviano Air Force Base and Camp Bondsteel both take five-kiloton strikes, although the shot over Aviano was kind of a dud.

Farther away in the Mediterranean, sea rats in their blue-and-white striped sailor shirts and gray helmets secure the cargo container that was the launch platform for the four cruise missiles that carried the underperforming ordnance. Created from scrap plastic and recycled computer parts and guided by GPS. technology cloned from sets stolen from department stores, our cruise missiles will punch brutal blows to the humans in their unsuspecting confusion. Produced in cottage industry shops from recycled waste and obsolete 'puters, the Dinosaurs' trash becomes our treasured war hammer. Even if our nuclear weapons are still just a little shoddy.

On a still, subzero, overcast afternoon in the wintery city of Saint Petersburg, history repeats itself as the winter palace, guarded by cute teenaged Russian girls in black uniforms and Kalashnikovs, form a defensive perimeter as rats carrying black banners and the Standard of Evolution flags scurry to the center of this historic place. Across the ocean, Mexico City burns in the morning twilight, as Havana fights off the combined efforts of the RLA on land, air, and sea. One land stays quite peaceful . . . the People's Republic of China, what we call the Great Green Dragon. In Beijing, emissaries of the Union toast our temporary Chinese friends, as Nixon did so long ago.

Livermore Labs sits still under the California winter night sky. Above it, on the flagpole that once bore the blue-, white-, and black-striped flag of these Dinosaurs, now holds our black Standard of Evolution. Inside the most secure section of the laboratory complex, the rats of the shock unit Lishek Chee 49 drop easily to the floor. Outside in the animal holding pens albino rats and mice, white traitors permanently corrupted by humanistic thought, lie where they were machine gunned down in their lab animal cages. Senior Shock Commander Guppy Trash scurries past cryogenized tanks of only Nature knows. Guppy uses his English reading skills to decipher the Dinosaurian script on the bottles.

"Shee!" squeals the hardened war rat in terror. "These things are filled with the Pestilence!"

"They've weaponized it already!" chirps his associate, Junior Commander Cheesy Pettingzoo. With this knowledge, the thrill of hammering humanity into extinction pours right out of every rat's spirit.

Even after eight thousand or so months, when the Pestilence killed a third of the Dinosaurs and only Nature knows how many of us, the terror of such a visitation upon Rodentia rests in the deepest crevices of our souls. Nature alone knows how many of the siblings still die each year from the Pestilence.

And if this isn't the only stockpile, the Dinosaurs just may take us with them if they commit species suicide.

The battle is joined by the damned. Outside of El Paso, cruise missiles blast out of their metal tubes on their way to slam into military targets a thousand clicks away. The launch tubes will take more cruise missiles, firing until the inventory runs out. By morning, hundreds of military targets across the Southwest will be destroyed. Nearby, eight-wheeled trucks, cloned from components taken from junkyards and diesel mechanics' shops, lift their multiple rocket launcher tubes into position. The rockets inside the tubes burn the earth near the trucks, clouding them with its smoke and aroma of cordite and pyrotechnics. In minutes, the rockets will drop by the hundreds on the prissy, comfortable suburbs and wretched habitats in front of the 138th Armored Shock Army, rolling unopposed by any organized or armed opposition.

Within the very heart of the universal city of humanity, the Five Burrows, the throng stops at Times Square as another mass of siblings joins them coming northwest on 42nd Street. Over a million of our siblings, rats, house mice, squirrels, and others converge at this location where a crew of the enemy had just finished cleaning this space for us. On the northeast corner, the long Banner of Liberation, a hundred foot strip of black muslin with white Rodentic letters proclaiming evolution's fulfilment and the All Rodents Evolutionary Union's triumph, unfurls down to the roof of an NYPD station. Beneath it, Associate Secretary Bunny Blackstone holds a megaphone in one paw, and a long strip of paper in the other. The ratty secretary reads the proclamation of the new epoch of Nature from the Big Cheese himself with sanctimonious faith in the Union, the Big Cheese, and Nature's destiny. Then he asks the crowd what song they should sing. They squeak out for that most beloved of anthems! So the band begins. The throng joins in with a rousing rendition of "Rodentia, Universal and Triumphant":

> *We bond together in sacred unity*
> *We will strive together 'til all the Earth is free*
> *We are one omni-species with the whole planet as our habitat*
> *The Scourge of Humanity, whether man, woman, or cat*
> *The Savior of Nature, the emancipator of the Earth*
> *On we go 'til the whole Earth is free*
> *We scamper triumphantly to the glorious victory*

Meanwhile, at the supreme command post twenty-seven clicks away to the north, the early reports come in to Comrade Steely.

"Over one hundred thousand mice deserted already, and there are reports of some mice and rats firing on RLA fighters," a Dzumban laments.

"Comrade Steely, we may have over a dozen of our divisions joining the Co-Operative Leagues . . ." Another Dzumban chirps out, only to be interrupted.

"Siblings! We mice are mice! Not men! Don't hold this desertion against us!" squeaks the house mouse Executive Secretary for Habitat, Gouda Eepsheepsheepshrk.

With a slap of his tail to the floor, Comrade Steely stands up. "Shut up. Both of you!" Silence draws all attention to the Big Cheese. "They turned on us! They couldn't have done this on their own." Our elder statesrat squats in contemplation.

"I just knew somebody would pull a stunt like this. Comrade Pike!"

Pike, the faithful and loyal lapdog, scurries up to Steely. "Comrade Steely. I am ready to serve!"

"Brother," Steely responds, relaxing his grip on the bad news. "You are the tomcat of evolution. Please take care of this."

## Chapter Six

# NATURE AGAINST HUMANITY

L os Angeles. To us: Lah, the City of the Desolation Angels. In the first hours of Year Zero, the intersection of the Century Freeway and I-110 burns from three propane tanks dropped on it from one of the thirty-eight dirigibles aloft in the stratosphere that were manufactured by us under the Earth. Along the Los Angeles River, modular homes and suburbia's habitat burn from bottles filled with napalm hitting them by the hundreds, dropped from our warbirds—the ones we affectionately named black swans.

Darkness smothers this city of light. And a concrete command post for the city's crisis management fills with the human chiefs of stability. A thousand meters above, Senior Air Rat Courage Cheeshchetey, a flying squirrel from the Midworst, points his right wing at the post filled with city leaders.

"Star Shine, this is Moonbeam! Target identified! Begin attack!" he calls.

From the night sky, close enough to the stars that they are visible, the flock of warbirds under Courage's command pounce on the command post. Bombs made from fire extinguishers and recycled plastic let inertia be their guide to the brain of the urban organism that is Lah. The whistling siren inspires the air rats, yet its frequency goes unnoticed by the Dinosaurs in their crosshairs. Courage pulls his warbird up to find a place in the heavens where he can observe the delivery. Like an expectant father. The target folds into the burning earth as the explosions give way to the subsequent fires consuming the vehicles parked around the one-time nerve center of the city's defense. Now Lah will fall decapitated, quivering in its death throes.

On the other side of the North American continent, lines of school buses filled with confused, traumatized newly homeless residents of a burning neighborhood make their way to a concentration camp set up by the recently activated Federal Emergency Management Administration. Overhead, flying in mottled gray liveries with jet motors on the tops of the fuselages behind the canopies, the warbirds of the Volunteers for Victory circle above the convoy, ready to fulfill their greatest mission. In the cockpit of the lead aircraft, Senior Airman Longsewer pulls the controls of his bird as he brings all his attention to bear on the lead bus. Over his plastic helmet a black headband with white rodent script written across it exclaims our mantra, "Rhu Ski Chew!" Glorious Victory! Without radios in any of their Hetsh 169 warbirds, he communicates with the other pilots through wing wagging. Longsewer points his left wing toward the line of buses and bounces his aircraft up and down to signal the attack. The jets peel out of formation toward the buses accelerating as they line up on the boxy yellow targets filled with the defenseless. As the targets fill the crude crosshairs, each pilot squeals the familiar cry of those who give the ultimate sacrifice.

"Rhu Ski Chew!" A dozen shrieking voices give way to deafening thunder as the buses explode from the impact of the live-guided cruise missiles.

In Ohio, North Dakota, and Michigan, over thirty-nine thousand airborne fighters parachute in air drops only to find confusion when they land, searching for each other and their equipment. And across the Earth, improvised explosive devices detonate, hosing the humans with scrap screws and glass shards. Our thousands of sniper guns attack soft targets (read: innocent, defenseless humans), spreading terror as one of our most effective force multipliers.

We play the first of our cards against humanity. That stink-species reels like a dipsomaniac. One foot in the grave, and both fists in the fight. Totally unpredictable.

In all, we surf the wave of Nature's destiny as our successful first strike shocks the body of that ol' reptile, humanity. But let's look at the scale of damage. Will our enemy simply chirp, "Ouch?" Will we need to be patient as they bleed to death? Or will the remnant rebuild?

Chapter Seven

# FROM THE CAPSTONE

*ewer tunnel under the city. Any human city across the burning, frozen winter landscape of Ayreka Orka, what the Dinosaurs call North America. As Dzumbani dressed in their best and cleanest service uniforms gather around a trophy case lit with liberated Christmas and desk lights, a special crew of rats with white cotton gloves pushes a bust of Comrade Steely into the case. From now on the passersby in the sewer will bow to the bust, in honor of the Husband of Nature, whose marriage ceremony is the Sacred War for Evolution, commenced Night One, Year Zero.*

I scurry through the liberated railroad station in what was Denver. At my side, three locomotives idle, waiting to ship our young fighters to the battlefield. Black banners hang along the sides of the cars. In front of the boilers of each of the locomotives sits a large portrait of the Big Cheese, framed by three black flags on each side, and wreathed with garlands of plastic flowers. Steam from the locomotives gently flows over my body with a delicious, indescribable sensation of comfort.

Young rats in battle dress squat on the platform all around me, backpacks full as a pregnant mama's belly ready to deliver. Rice tubes and bedrolls wrap around their torsos. Slung over their shoulders, they bear rifles, submachine guns, or those squad automatic machine guns with the funny-looking furniture. I always remember those as the weapons with the barrels that overheat too easily. These young tomcats of evolution squat pressed together with their loved ones, their pups and parents, grandmothers, and sex buddies, all sharing the pain of imminent separation. Rodentia will win, but will these young heroes, the greatest of our species, live to enjoy victory and reconstruction? Will they be wholly changed? The sweet sorrow of parting cannot be washed away by anything.

The steam clouds drift over mothers smelling their pups possibly for the last time. Couples rub their whiskers together. Fathers keep their sadness inside, hidden by facades of pride and honor. It is essential for the males to be the emotional pillars at a time like this.

Near the middle loading platform, a squeaker blares out the virtues of the New Natural Rodent, embodied by the semimythical figure of Comrade Senior Fighter Spunky Li Fungusmungoosa. Under the squeaker, a family gathers, one of the millions across the Union bidding farewell to the fruit of their wombs. Mother Moonbeam Chripsshrpl, with her fourth litter at home in the nest, sniffs the oldest of her offspring. Her firstborn, Senior Fighter Long Grass Chripsshrpl, squats stoically on the outside, but inside he feels the pain of this parting in the soul of his mother. At the nearby Regional Militia Forces post, he was commissioned as a lishek leader, with over forty fighters under his command. His two brothers, Fighters Bat Face and Weasel, fresh from their one-month basic and two-week advanced artillery trainings, squat wearing freshly pressed green uniforms. Made from fiberglass threads and polyethylene shellac, their new helmets sit attached to their backpacks, over their little shovels. All three sons try to comfort their mother. She's already lost two pups to disease. Ferret, her beloved beau rat, just last week was killed and eaten by a feral cat. The uncertainty torments her more than anything. Yet she isn't alone. Her firstborn daughter, Senior Fighter Ferocious, a girl rat demolitions expert with the Regional Militia Forces, squats by her side. Ferocious will be stationed within scurrying distance of her mother, so she can still help raise the others. But at any moment, Nature might call her away to fight humans.

The steam clouds lift, then the whistle from the first locomotive calls for final boarding. Green army uniforms and blue laborers' work clothes divide into two masses as the fighters congregate at the doors of the railroad cars. As final farewells whistle out of the open windows of the cars, the war trains pull out, as they do across the Union, across the species, in one way or another, across Earth. In the souls of the loved ones, paying the price as a holy sacrifice to the great cause of evolution will never remotely yield a return on their investment.

I haven't found anything about the Mystery Girl Rat. Was she, in fact, a fairy? Maybe I created her in my imagination under the delicious stress of combat. As I ponder this, our cheebahs fly down to take my mobile staff of a dozen rodents along with me back to the Central Command and Control Center in the mountains. Once aboard our aluminum dragonflies, we strap ourselves to the interiors, then into the air we go. I used to love the stream of air blowing on me from the outside, but I ignore it now as I ball up on the floor. The vibration of the aircraft lulls me to sleep.

Someone bites me, and I attack like a cornered rat.

"No, Comrade Fearless! It's your assistant."

I bristle up at the form, sniffing the threat, assessing it. But I smell the unmistakable pheromone of my de facto valet, Cat Claw, so I back down.

Cat Claw earned my respect when I read his dossier. Combat veteran in our brushfire wars against the Co-Operative Leagues. Union member for fifty months. Most of that dedicated to service, within and outside of our Union's service structure. Cat Claw went from some rathole in the Bay Area to the corridors of power as a servant, a fighter, a member in good standing of our Union. We proudly share the same species, being two of the Shriedaygahbayan. Yet I feel I still must prove myself to him as his superior. And he has my respect, but not my trust, as of yet.

"Comrade Cat Claw, thank you so much for waking me."

"I apologize if my means seemed a bit threatening," Comrade Cat Claw replies. In the interest of amends-making, he pulls his body away from mine.

"Don't worry about it," I squeak as we hop out of the cheebah. "I should've stayed awake."

After landing, we enter the Command and Control Room. Around the circular perimeter, a circle of telephone operators behind telecommunications equipment squabble in microphones as the war effort continues on the other ends of the party lines. I set up the business of evolution's imperative at the command table. A second or three of prework gnawing on the table, and I attack my tasks as if they were cowering

Dinosaurs in the crosshairs of my weapon. I sniff around under the table and can't find my earphones.

"Cat Claw! Where are my earphones?" I squeal.

"You took them with you on Night Minus One!" comes the reply.

"Bug thorner!" I hit my head on the table as I crawl out from underneath. "Well, I'll just have to improvise. RegIntel!" I order to our facilitator of the regional information.

Across the room, the intelligence chief of the Rocky Mountain region, Comrade Executive Regional Intelligence Commander Cheddar Wee Wheechiskachee squeals in a mousy voice that slices through the boiler room chatter, "Comrade! Please call me on your headset!"

"Comrade Wee! In five minutes, give me an update on our status!" goes my order.

"Comrade Fearless, with all respect, would you please follow your own protocol!" comes his insubordination.

"Brother Wee! Would you be so inclined as to lead a Volunteers for Victory battalion into a well-defended bunker filled with human fighters?" I politely threaten.

The mouse doesn't understand my Shrie accented Ratsqueak any better than I get his insolence. Add in the fact that he is a house mouse, and you can't get more arrogant than that.

Comrade Cat Claw saves the day as he approaches me with my very own headset. I sniff it out and calm down as I take it out of his mouth. Once on, the headset's jill goes into the right jack. Or maybe it's the other way around if you think about it.

"Brother Wee! Stand at attention!" I command, once again the alpha of the Rockies.

"Sir!" squeaks the mouse, who then passes out. Or did he just drop dead from fright?

Security elements gather around him, all Shries with sub-machine guns strapped to their backs, and clean, crisply pressed light green uniforms on their fury bodies. The arrogant mouse revives, then contritely whistles over the set.

"Comrade Executive Commander Fearless! Please forgive me!" comes his apology.

I forgive him for the moment, but something's afoot, I believe.

As the morning approaches, I gnaw and piss everywhere in anticipation of my dinner. The major Dinosaur airport west of the city smolders under its snowy surface. We've already declared the airport disinfested of humans, only to have more of those shaved monkeys pop out of their subterranean hiding places. Kill one human, and five pop up out of the earth to take its place. Under the airport, we have already found over a dozen layers of tunnels. Nature only knows how many meters deep those reptiles have their shelters. I read a report the night before last that we killed a human that measured *four and a half meters* in length! Tunnel giant.

The jarring beep of the public address system arrests my attention, pulling it from my appetite. I turn my ears and muzzle to the set of squeakers sitting over the entry to the Command and Control Room. It is that familiar blend of two black ears on a round stand, providing both stereophonic sound and listening. We can be heard as clearly as we can hear the PA system.

"Attention! Attention! Your attention, please! Stand by for the direct and live species-wide address from our own alpha of alphas!" The central information network has our attention, but then we get that crappy boring music made by beetles. Thank Grand Mother Nature that it's in reverse.

The annoying music ends with a moment of silence, followed by the introduction of our GenSec, who begins the weekly All Rodents Collective Conscience Meeting that is heard across radio waves and streamed into every rodent's i-stuff.

"Comrades, siblings, citizens of the All Rodents Evolutionary Union . . . Comrade Steely squeaks!" The second moment of silence. Then . . .

"Comrades, siblings, citizens of the All Rodents Evolutionary Union . . . ," comes the high-pitched nasally voice of our leader, the Big Cheese. So original and unique! "Soon morning will fall across our hemisphere. Comrade Steely squats here among spiritual giants and ever-eager beavers of service to our Union. You members gathered here in this hallowed Great Hall of all us rodents . . ."

Over three thousand clicks away, in the central space of what once was the New York Botanical Gardens, the Big Cheese opens the first weekly meeting of the All Rodents Evolutionary Standing Committee, bathed in the aromatherapeutic effect of so many different flowers. Within this newly named Great Hall of Evolution, his powerful words reverberate across the hall as the assembled committee members and council representatives numbering into the thousands sit in attention taking in his wisdom.

"To you, faithful and trustworthy general service representatives of our Union, from your home lisheks to this assembly, you are the real leaders of our Union." A tentative applause breaks out. "Thank you." Silence. "And thank you for your service to our species." Another tentative applause. "Your Comrade Steely proposes tonight this new doctrine of War Collectivism. We're embroiled in this terrible struggle, which is as much a struggle for unity as it is anything. So I bring forth Executive Proposal #00319. 'A proposal adapting the policy and practice of the doctrine of War Collectivism.'"

In five minutes, he presents this doctrine intended to guide the Union in its righteous war of extermination of all of Nature's enemies. Unanimously adopted by the grateful assembly, the precepts of War Collectivism include the following policies:

The Species Production Board will hereby be named the Central Species Planning Board.

All industry will be centralized. Strict centralized management will be introduced under the Central Species Planning Board.

All labor, already organized under the Species Production Planning Board, will be subject to the Rodents Liberation Army's Discipline and Order Pronouncement of Dinosaur Night October 2, 2013.

Central, collective control and management of trade within the species will be introduced.

Under the Central Species Planning Board, discipline for all fighters, laborers, and gardeners will be, and must be strict. Absolutely no strikes will be allowed, nor tolerated.

Obligatory labor duty will be imposed onto non-working social stations.

Obligatory war service duty will be required for those fulfilling labor duty.

Requisition of all horticultural surpluses from gardeners in ex-
    cess of absolute minimum will be conducted for centralized
    distribution among the remaining population. "Absolute
    minimum" will be determined by the Executive Office of the
    Central Species Planning Board.

All essential commodities, including time, information, food, raw
    materials, and precious metals, will be considered property
    of the All Rodents Evolutionary Union, so that it can be dis-
    tributed fairly and most usefully. Food and most commodi-
    ties will be distributed in urban centers in a centralized way.

Knowledge, known in its raw element as "data," will hereby be
    deemed the most essential and volatile commodity. There-
    fore, all means of distributing information, recording infor-
    mation, and displaying information, will rest in the paws
    of the All Rodents Evolutionary Union, to be produced, dis-
    tributed, displayed and shared according to the dictates of
    military and security necessity. All means of communication
    and recording, including but not exclusive to, photography
    equipment, video equipment, typewriters, and any device
    that processes words, will be the property of the Union, and
    will never be allowed in the paws of the proletariat without
    expressed permission and consent. A Central Office of Nat-
    ural Information will be tasked with fulfilling the above.

The correct and proper interpretation of all data will be the
    exclusive privilege of the AREU, through established com-
    mittees of the Central Species Planning Board.

Social class structure and hierarchy will hereby be eliminated,
    replaced by rank and echelon.

Private enterprise will become illegal.

Private ownership of property will be the sole privilege of the
    AREU. All of Nature's bounty will be recognized as the
    property of the Union as a whole, to be held and distributed
    by the Central Species Planning Board.

The AREU hereby institutes military control of railways, air
    travel, and shipping. Logistics will be fulfilled through a
    new element of the Rodents Liberation Army, the Logistics
    Units.

The newly formed All Rodents Extraordinary Commission will
    bear the task of policing and disciplining the Union mem-
    bership. This Commission will answer directly to the office
    of the GenSec.

"With this centralizing of control over the lives of the
siblings, the hopes of all rodents will be met in this show of
unity," our GenSec concludes, humble in his power and dominance. And yet, Nature forbid anyone hear my soul's ponder-
ing, but this all sounds as fishy as a school of guppies to me.

## Chapter Eight

# TEAM SPIRIT

A week later, the meeting takes on a more somber tone. Our leader squats once again before the assembly, with a full register roll that bears the names of so many of our colleagues. At the ready, throughout the auditorium, squat members of the newly-founded All Rodents Extraordinary Commission, RODEXCOM to the most privileged, or simply RexCom to everyone else.

"Siblings," begins Steely. "The list I bring before you today includes the threats to evolution that come from the dangerous and selfish rightist path of individuality. We know we've never smelled an individual beat a team yet. We are the team; the individual is responsible for submission to the extrinsic focus of the collective need and purpose of the order and the Union. All of us stands important, each of us is expendable."

In unison, the three thousand or so gathered squeak out the rhythmic chant "Rhu Ski Chew" in a cadence punctuated by the thumping of their tails on the floor. As Steely tries to continue, the rhythm gains momentum, overpowering the magnitude of his personality. Then the auditorium quiets down, momentarily.

A voice from the crowd exclaims, "Forever live the Big Cheese's power and majesty!" The rhythm starts anew. Steely bears himself with appreciation, but annoyance as well.

Then another joins in before the throng gets too quiet. "Forever lives the wisdom of our most heroic Big Cheese!" The rhythm renews itself, irritating the honored and celebrated alpha rat.

"Forever lives our First Sibling's leadership!" As the rhythm of the worship takes on a new, stronger thunder, Steely hisses at them, puffing his fur up in agitation. He beats the podium with his tail, to regain his own dominance.

"Brother Comrade Steely would like to squeak a few things, now!" hisses Steely. The sound doesn't change. "Shut up and let me squeak!" The unstoppable applause quiets down quickly, to dead silence. "Siblings! Comrades! This is the hardest thing I may ever do as your GenSec. This list begins where all real change and improvement must. Among us . . . And no applause until I'm done!" More silence. Like a tomb of those resting in peace. "Among us tonight, spies, traitors to our species, slackers, and seditious workers against Nature sit in our midst . . ." Discomfort sets in. Fur goes up the backs of Union members. ". . . Shoulder to shoulder with you. Yes, you! Your comrade. Your neighbor. Your fellow laborer. Your brother. Your sister. Your father. Maybe even your pups!" The rodents in attendance chatter their teeth, afraid to make a false move. "The enemy may sit next to you, squirming in guilty fear." This gets the audience to freeze. Yet ready to vibrate like a jumping bean.

Steely unfurls the register roll. Filled with names of perceived enemies, the roll travels down to the front row of service members. With a paw on each edge of the paper, Steely
begins the reading of the Enemies List. He gets to one, then
pauses strategically, followed with his chirpy mourning over
such imagined betrayal. "Tite Squerlaway . . . Brother, you
were more of an elder statesrat than I. Why?"

"Brother!" pleads the pack rat. "I never betrayed you . . .
What did I do?" RexCom fighters take the aging pack rat's
shoulder. As RexCom security elements drag him out with his
pressed uniform in their jaws, he repeats the query, "What did
I do?" Steely wipes his muzzle in bitter sorrow, then gnaws
mournfully on the pulpit.

"Let the Big Cheese be our elder statesrat!" squeaks a
Union faithful. Others squeal the favorite slogan, then they
fall silent with Steely's whistle.

"This is killing me. Torturing me . . . Kchirkee Peanutbut-
ter . . ." Steely sorrowfully chirps all the more as a fox squirrel
flicks his tail in terror, leaping away in a desperate scamper.
RexCom fighters apprehend him, along with others. "Siblings!
How could anyone called a friend do such a thing against our
own Grand Mother Nature?"

"Execute them!" shrieks a rat in the back.

"Feed 'em to the ferrets!" squeals another.

"Nuke 'em in the microwave!" commands a Dzumban
in the back row. The meeting erupts in the rhythmic chant,
"Nuke 'em!"

Steely chatters in rage. "Shut up and let me finish!" Silence.

Steely continues until the list is read. Then he stops and
looks out at the assembly. "Comrades. Brothers. I could never
agree with our former doctrinarian, Comrade Sheep Poker
on some things. There is no synthesis, like he always claimed.

And now I have every good reason to believe he is the prime suspect in this horrible plot to take over our universally shared collective leadership. The former doctrinarian, archivist, comrade, member of the Union . . . Eech Sheep Poker, is an enemy of the species!"


"Nature! Capstone! Species! These are the watchwords that gather all of us, from the many, into the one unified All Rodents Evolutionary Union. Underlying these words, the truer watchwords of superorganism, meme, and hierarchy . . . ," the blah-blah-blah of the mechanical herald of the capstone challenges our souls with a lot of negative inspiration. And with religious faith and childish trust, my fellow rodents surrender their ears to the black-eared transmitters.

I scurry under that silly apparatus with the Mickey Mouse Club ears, thinking about the "Steely Rat Club." Young fighters of the Steel Youth Brigades scurrying into the point of view. Each one answers the roll call with a single name.

"Sleaze Ball!"

"Spunky!"

"Kitty Thorner!"

"Spunky!"

"Annette!"

A good third of pups across the Union get the name "Spunky!" Catnip and I will name our thirty pups something original! To think Nature's future rests on the shoulders of these tailed dynamos attired in pressed white cotton tunics, no trousers, and the regulation black bandana around their collars. And between their ears, they always wear the kepi, that familiar cap worn by fighter and worker, with the bill, the strip of fabric on the front, and three tiny holes on each side, part of the uniform of all Union members. For RexCom, the kepi is always black, so we call those bugs Black Caps.

I smell a human in all of this. The service structure of our Union shifts from a triangle on its point, to a pyramid resting on its foundation, and the capstone separating itself from the mass. We're meant to have the lishek, that unit of rodents that we live together in, be the highest unit of authority within the Union. The General Service Office, GenSerOff as we know it, has always been the servant to the lisheks. That's the basis of our service structure. Foundation down to our GenSerOff. Under Steely, the GenSerOff becomes the capstone. Yet it is quite natural in its own right to have a head ruling a body.

This is how it works in nature. Making up every organism are three components: meme, hierarchy, and the superorganism. Each covers the trinity of existence: body, soul, and spirit. Meme, the soul component, wraps itself around the idea, passion-scape, and will of the superorganism. The physical aspect of an organism is the mass, or body, but I like to say mass. The masses that constitute the Union are collectively, the Masses. The social, spiritual aspect (the two are synonymous, if you think about it) governs each mass, each soul, each organism, driving them together into an order that will preserve the superorganism. Call it the spirit, life energy of the organism, or qi, that either progresses, or else the superorganism regresses to extinction.

"Eech Sheep Poker has escaped to the high desert!" comes over the PA. "Our beloved Leader personally has signed an arrest warrant for him! Citizen! Sibling! Yes, you, my brother! My sister! You have all authority from the Big Cheese to make a citizen's arrest when you smell him! If you don't, you'll be considered an accomplice to his treason!"

I sniff around myself. Cat Claw is nowhere to be found. He was just by my side a few minutes ago. I have a war to win, so he'll have to catch up with me later. But I wonder about him.


An hour later, I bounce around in the hatch of my su-sto as we, the cat fur–dressed liberators of the Earth, scamper through the streets of Centennial, Colorado. Sunlight invades the horizon and could quite possibly betray our location. Buildings burn around us. Shots ring out from a few straggling Dinosaurs with varmint rifles. That Dinosaur militia, the Colorado National Guard, lobs mortar bombs at us. Their whistles precede the crash of thunderous explosions behind our armored spearhead. Missed us! Missed us! Now you gotta kiss us!

Our turretless tank charges over the snowy asphalt flanked by submachine gun-bearing eight-wheeled rigs. We roll past the frozen bodies of Dinosaurs lying scattered about the sidewalks. On the tops of the hulls of our iron war horses we proudly fly black banners in the breeze, banners calling for unity of the brethren and destruction of all negative elements of Nature. Supplemented with metal sheets, strips from tires and plywood scraps, the white-washed armor of our vehicles bear statements such as "For Rodentia!" "For the Big Cheese!" "All Glory to the Fighters and Liberators of the Rocky Mountain Front!" From the pock-marked soot-stained shell of a dormitory of some liberated college campus flies a banner declaring "All Rodents are Fighters! All Fighters are Liberators!" Resistance from the enemy fills the snow-packed gutters of the streets with our martyrs, our dead. Left behind in the snow, physically, but together with us in spirit.

At an intersection, the Regimental Constabulary, wearing their white leather Sam Browne belts and gloves, shrieks orders at us through megaphones made from Dixie Cups. These aren't the pretty prairie dogs of York Street, but a half dozen hefty, well-fed Dzumbani who hate us Shries more that they hate humanity.

"Twenty-third Brigade to the east! Forty-fifth Route Army to the west!" come the commands from those keepers of military peace and speciesist conflict.

One sniffs the air my way, wiggling his whiskers in disgust. "Phew! Is that stink what I think it is, fellows?"

Another adds his treason against Rodentia with, "Ick! Stinks like a Nature-damned Jeemsh to me. A whole cat box full of 'em!"

The Dzumbani laugh at these insults, like immature pups mocking a new pup in the schoolyard.

"You're squeaking at the executive commander of the Rocky Mountain Strategic Direction!" I chirp viciously at them.

"Don't confuse your rank with our authority!" one of them chirps back, with cold, self-righteous pseudo-authority. Another waves his little black-and-white flags at us, ordering us to stop.

I grab my throat microphone. "Keep moving!"

Our column rolls past these species-ists, who puff up their fur against us, hissing and pissing at us the filthiest verbal poison I've ever heard. One scurries to a clipboard and scribbles something. I'm surprised an ignoramus like this species-ist isn't illiterate. Most rodents are. Despite our "Rodents Read and Write" campaign.

We've liberated an industrial park west of the big airport. From underneath its burned surface, humans still pop up out of its rubble to hit us. I scurry into a shop with a long placard hanging over its open door. I hear the whistle and clack-clack-clack of an incoming mortar round, likely flying in from the airport. Its report hits my ears as the shock wave from the explosion caresses me, just for a second.

We put together enough tools and machinery in this machine shop to rebuild the thousands of cars and trucks we took from the humans. Across the wall in the rear of the open space, another long placard hangs from the roof. Under it, another of those two-eared listening/broadcasting devices blares out reports of some successful three-month plan, with all the statistics repeated as if we all want to know the number of tons of food waste we've turned into explosives, or some confusing statistic like that. In front of it, surrounded by garlands of fresh flowers (in winter? When we can't get fresh veggies?), a marble bust of our elder statesrat, Steely, the Big Cheese, stands as an idol. The Big Cheese smells everything. I look for the first aid class my lovebug, Catnip, plans to lead. Her aroma enters my muzzle, and comfort bathes my body and soul. That pheromone can slice through the smell of grease and shop chemicals like a razor through soft skin.

Catnip and another nurse squat by a first aid kit as a whole lishek of about forty rodents gathers around. A cell of seven Dzumbani females scurries up to the kit. I barely see their uniform patches featuring a crescent moon on the bottom of a black disk. These are retrievers, golden retrievers to any of our siblings saved under fire by their courage and self-sacrifice.

Maybe they know the Mystery Girl Rat? I scurry up to them as one takes her place by my delicious Catnip. Here they are, a Shrie senior trauma nurse and a Dzumban trauma medical technician, squatting side by side, in unity. No speciesism to be smelled. This smells like . . . victory! Unity is victory. Speciesism equals defeat. Anyway, I smell the Dzumban by my girl rat's side, and a memory flows through my soul.

The Dzumban takes charge of the first aid class. "Comrades! Siblings!" she chips with authority. "Let's get this class going. I am Senior Retriever Cappuccino of the RLA Medical Organ. You're all going to learn how to save your sibling or yourself because the whole planet is now a battlefield. And as laborers? You're just as likely to get wounded in combat as any of your fighter siblings . . ."

The lady knows her stuff. And she's right. We're all fighters. Combat can come to this workshop with a counter assault from humanity. She continues as Catnip assists her, but through the presentation, I get the impression that I found that Girl Rat.

The class wraps up. I approach this girl Dzumban who now has a name. "Comrade Cappuccino," I purr, then sniff her tail hole in the familiar greeting of rats with a familiar fellow. She slams her tail to tell me we're not that familiar. I back away, taking a neutral stance.

"We don't know each other, do we?" she shrieks at me.

"Comrade. I think we met on the battlefield a few weeks ago," I share, hoping I come to her mind.

"I just rotated out of three weeks of combat duty, and I don't need some Inner Union stinkbug I don't know sniffing my privy parts!"

Diplomacy, quick! "I sincerely apologize for the offense," I offer, "But I got to tell you. Ever since we saved a brother from a burning tank, you've been in my soul, and I want . . . would really like to have you on my staff. At least we could interview each other first. We could get an idea if we're compatible." At least, she listens to me. But she doesn't really soften.

"I have my assignment. After all, you don't want a bossy girl on your staff. You'd hate the competition, I'm sure."

Before I can come up with some more witty repartee, the PA system whistles out that annoying and shrill call to attention.

"Attention! Attention! Your attention, please!" the system blares. "Stand by for an essential and mandatory announcement from the Elder Statesrat Executive Office." When it's "Essential and mandatory," it's now illegal to scurry away somewhere else.

Bugles toot out the warning call from the PA system. Maybe a whole orchestra blowing their trumpets. The voice of a brother rat with that Dzumban growl in his voice follows. "Comrades! Siblings! Builders and fighters! Please listen! The trial of the West Texas Twelve is about to begin!"

All of us pay attention despite the boring drone of lies coming across the mouse-eared squeakers. How could a clique of Texas mice and rats (and one armadillo, who can't even read or write) be such a threat to the whole All Rodents Evolutionary Union, which stretches across the Earth? One of the squeaking collaborators drones on, then adds, ". . . I was deranged. I had lost all smell of the richness of the Big Cheese's pheromone, and instead fell under the hypnosis of Eech Sheep Poker . . ." A gasp comes from our audience.

A gerbil dressed in cat fur and a starched and stiff-collared officer's uniform nips at my thigh. "Fearless. I remember you from the Ninth International. You insulted our glorious leader!"

Another hears this and demands, "Who insulted our Big Cheese?"

"I am your commanding officer! Don't gossip!" I shriek.

"Comrade Steely is our supreme commander! And he's under attack!" comes a voice from the group.

"Just shut the thorn up and listen!" Comrade Cappuccino squeals. Then she sniffs at me with suspicion. "Are you a good comrade or a stinky Jeemsh?" she asks.

I turn to her and wiggle my whiskers at her. "Comrade. Quiet!" She turns away silently, but I feel her vibration. Anyone can be a soul criminal. Even me. But never her.

## Chapter Nine

# ENEMIES OF THE SPECIES

Across our beloved Rodentia, the computer monitors fill with the breaking news. On the screens, Chief Prosecutor Dzinka Dzeebeediyah stands at a podium. He shakes with religious rancor as he interrogates the enemies of our species, the voice of our capstone in its quest to purge itself of the poisonous waste product within our superorganism's head. In front of his podium, other siblings squat at tables with their whole attention on him. He chirps out a thunderous squeak, lower than the average rodent voice. Comrade Prosecutor Dzeebeediyah wears that familiar uniform of our new elite, the stiff-collared jacket with three pockets we're all coming to recognize as the dzash. Four pockets show the wearer belongs to the elite of the elite. Over the left breast pocket he wears some civilian achievement metals along with a platinum metal in the Big Cheese's likeness.

"And furthermore! Sheep Poker's adherence to the fallacious doctrine of synthesis as an integral part of the Cheddarbreathian Dialect opposes our glorious boss's . . ." With that, Dzeebeediyah turns toward a bust of the Big Cheese and bows his head respectfully, joined by everybody else, with the exception of the guards, who all stand at attention in their crisply starched and pressed uniforms. ". . . Interpretation of the dialectic, that there are only two—thesis, and antithesis—causing all Nature to be driven by conflict, conflict, and more conflict . . ."

Within nights, a dark story of mythical proportions emerges in our species-controlled media. Apparently, in our very midst, enemies against our new GenSec have been conspiring to undermine his authority with the express purpose of stealing out of the paws of Steely the very reins of power over our beloved Union. Muzzles of the confessing traitors appear.

"The Sheep Poker Clique grew from out of the vile mind our scheming leader, Eech. I personally crawled up the Dinosaur's ass, and achieved the greater organism, by serving the Poker!" confesses the gerbil Skeekhec Pewpewpew, former associate doctrinarian of the Executive Commissariat of Ideology.

"I licked the cat's asshole and called it symbiosis. I was deranged," confesses the Dzumban co-conspirator Bunny Dzeem Gshveely, one-time general service steward in charge of political correctness within the RLAAF Central Command.

The confessions flash on the computer monitors. Squeal out over the central radio squeakers. Blare from posters and headlines. But nowhere do we see Sheep Poker actually confessing to anything. Where is he?

I never would have dreamed that my dear friend in service, Eech Sheep Poker, was an enemy. I always knew him as a servant to the common good. And he didn't threaten the superorganism with any individualistic thinking or feelings. I think for myself, as a service to Rodentia. That's why I study Co-operative Thought. The Co-operative Leagues north of us survive well despite our unjust war to annihilate them. I don't see them as a threat or competition, but rather as a resource. An example: Their communities operate as sovereign entities. They remain autonomous, except in matters affecting other communities, or the league as a whole. If one whole league fails, the others can survive. Not so with our new collectivization. But for the good of the whole, I'll pocket my pride, sublimate my critical thinking, and agree with the faith of the masses.

## Chapter Ten

# NINE MINUTES OF LOVE

The thousand or so of we rodents watching the screen flinch when the aggravating, dry squeal of a fan belt reverberates through the warehouse. Our delicate ears writhe in pain from the racket, put through a liberated eight-track sound mixer. The screen shows images of road-killed gophers, squirrels shot with .410 shotguns for a stew pot, mice caught in traps. A transformer burns as a squirrel's tail whips around, then goes limp. Then images of pollution, over-population, clear-cutting, and nuclear power plants flash on the screen, superimposed with the bust of the evil Bard himself. That terrible doctrinarian of Dinosaurian humanistic thought William Shakespeare set the stage for our planet's death with his lies. As a sister reads it out loud, a quote from his propaganda tome he named *Hamlet* appears in white, printed in the characters of our writing system.

". . . What a piece of work is man! How noble in reason! How infinite in faculty! In form and moving how express and admirable! In action how like an angel! In apprehension how like a god! The beauty of the world! The paragon of the animals . . . !"

A rat wearing a factory worker's uniform with bandoliers and a rifle around his shoulder breaks into the screen through the characters.

"Siblings! Don't you believe it!" he whistles.

In front of liberated computer monitors, we rodents, workers, gardeners, bureaucrats, and Inner Union members gather in our places as the Nine-Minute Love Celebration of the Big Cheese begins. On the screens, Chief Prosecutor Dzinka Dzeebeediyah stands at a podium, shaking with religious rancor. In front of his podium, other siblings squat at tables with their whole attention on him.

"Comrades, siblings, fighters, and laborers!" Chief Dzinka chirps. "Our whole universe rests on the ratty shoulders of one rat, our beloved and trusted Comrade Steely! Never before in natural history has so much depended on so little! Against him, cliques of the unseen enemy conspire to steal his great work for their own selfish motives!" He bristles up as he addresses the court, slapping his tail on the ground as he scurries in front of the accused.

I, the very independent and personally sovereign Fearless Litzkachew, find myself actually wiggling my whiskers in agreement. The harangue gives way to the screens filling up with traitors, cowards, slackers, and spies for Argentina, the declared enemies of the species. Next to me, a Dzumban in her green girl rat's uniform looks to a Shrie next to her, a bureaucrat in slate blue overalls, the standard uniform of those millwrights of the machinery of state, the petty Union *apparatchiki.*

"Brother, please answer me . . . who is Argentina?" The inquiry to the bureaucrat is taken with suspicion.

"Is this some sort of species-ist thing?" he responds.

Another image appears. A mouse . . . no, not a mouse. An anthropomorphic pseudo-mousy lie masquerading as a mouse! And then another joins him. Both stand upright, like Dinosaurs in love. One wears Mickey Mouse boots, like the standard-issue winter boots worn by our siblings on the Rocky Mountain Front. The other wears a dress similar to a girl Dinosaur's. Superimposed over them, the mustachioed image of a pathetically happy, smiling older human that we know as Diz'ee appears. When two pseudo-squirrels show up, the chipmunks in the audience chirp with rancorous hostility, demanding the frozen head of Diz'ee on a platter of ice cream.

Again, another image shows up. Huge, oversize skeletons of reptiles, long extinct, stand in the Museum of Natural History. The viewpoint zooms into the skull of a Tyrannosaurus rex, accompanied by the sound of an ugly growl. Then the point of view goes to the skeleton of a human, then to that of a cat. Appearing over the image of a human skull is a picture of the image of Tcharlz Darzhi', who wrote the scatologic tome of lies on evolution *The Origins of Feces.*

Superimposed on the screen under Darzhi's visage, the standard Ratsqucak letters spell out "This is how your world will end, humanity. Not with a whimper, but with a squeak!"

The audience goes into hysterics at the loathing of these three. I join in with as much hostility as anyone. This is love! It feels good! As videos of the trials appear, we squeak out,

"Traitor! Soul criminal! Dinosaurian humanist!" at the top of
our lungs and from the bottom of our hearts.

The monitors go black and then come back alive with a
hissing sound. We flinch at the image of a big, mean-looking
Maine coon cat leaping into the point of view. Superimposed
over it, a second cat's face appears, opening its mouth with a
malignant meow. Then the image fades into the unmistakable
mug of the former doctrinarian and archivist, my ex-friend,
Eech Sheep Poker.

My fur stands up on my back. All my hormones flow
through my body, preparing me for battle. And I don't even
know where the bug-thorning Sheep Poker is.

The announcer drones on, completely drowned out by
our religious zeal. Then through the white noise of our united
voices his prodding cuts through to my attention. "Squeak,
squeak, squeak out his name!"

"Sheep Poker!" We squeal out his name with terror in our
collective voice. In the air, the stench of cat piss sends terror
anew through our souls. I don't know why I go along with all
this. But it's as though I don't want to resist this urge to join
the mob mentality. I feel swept into a channel where I will never be lonely. In this collective consciousness, I lose my sense
of identity, trading it in for membership in a power greater
than myself.

With a rhythmic drone of "meow, meow" accompanying
him, Sheep Poker rambles on in that southwestern scorpion
mouse accent of his, with its peeps and squeaks. "For the
Union has lost its moral compass under the leadership of this
new administration. The surrender of individual thought and
expression to the so-called collective good will end the natural
hierarchy of merit and talent and replace it with a miserable
hierarchy of personality.

"For the Union is now, in fact, individualistic. But the only individual of this individuality is . . ." At that, Sheep Poker's image turns into a roaring tomcat.

We are beside ourselves, perhaps actually enjoying our rejection of this heresy. And yet I can't disagree with any of my friends' points of view.

In the newly restored ventilation system, RexCom and Inner Union operatives open a bottle of airmarked alpha pheromone. Out flows the unmistakable smell of the Big Cheese, produced in a laboratory, and reproduced in the perfume factories of the Union. With his scent comes his image on the screen. Steely, the alpha rodent.

The audience puffs air again. The girl rat who earlier inquired about the spy Argentina and threw her personal copy of the fifth edition of the *Standard Ratsqueak Dictionary* at the ugly face of Diz'ee, now melts in relief seeing and smelling her savior. She joins us in a chorus in front of Steely's image. Together, we all chant that easily recognizable sound of the faithful. The chant echoes across the audience, the initials of the Big Cheese repeated in a hypnotizing chant, "Tay Shay, Tay Shay, Tay Shay . . ."


I don't know what it is. I experience a warm, cuddly feeling now for our glorious leader. Our elder statesrat gazes down at us from the honored places in every hovel, every intersection in our tunnel systems, and every corner of every liberated street. The tall photographs that hang on each street give us all a comfort, knowing our father figure is always present, even if we can't see them because we are so nearsighted. Good Comrade Steely is no absentee father, unlike most fathers in Rodentia. He inspires us all to take our holy war against humanity to the Dinosaurs' very heart and eat it out. Or make those two-legged, tailless reptiles do it themselves!

I pack up my combat kit with the blackboard in the expedient command post. Good comrade Cat Claw sterilizes the room by erasing the battle plans from the blackboard. Not sterilize, in the sense of germ cleaning, but in cleaning away any germ of information that can benefit our enemies.

I shoulder my pack with the battle plans and Cat Claw joins me, dressed up for a good early morning Dinosaur hunt. Behind us, our Dzumban brother Comrade Steely watches us. We scurry across the snow, quiet in our souls as we crawl into our cheebah. We strap in, and the whine of the rotary wings of our cheebah mesmerizes us, entrancing us, bringing our souls into our combat spirits. When we're over a herd of human swine, we will automatically become Death with long, naked tails. Senior bad tails and lovin' it!

## Chapter Eleven

# EXTRAORDINARY COMMISSION

The central meeting hall of the office of the All Rodents Extraordinary Commission vibrates along its floor with the activity of a full complement of officers, senior staff members, military commanders, and sycophants. Disproportionately but not entirely Dzumbani, the rodents in the meeting called by Steely sit in rapt attention. In order to look taller, fighting the insecurity over his diminutive size, Steely stands on a brick hidden from view. Steely came dressed in his white jacket, clean and pressed, with medals showing the Order of the Gold Sun, the Order of the Full Moon, Hero of the AREU, Guardian of Nature. He never served a night in the RLA, but wears the metals wherever he goes, more than most of the bravest, self-sacrificing fighters ever will. I have a few of those meaningless trinkets. Stashed away, somewhere.

With a whistle, Steely gets the attention of the whole group. "Siblings. Servants of Nature and our Union. Guardians of the Rodentian soul. Comrades. Your comrade Steely presents to you a list of threats and enemies to Nature. Threats to our species and order, and to our Union. Most of all, to you and me. Personally, I grieve the moral failings I see in the hearts of others who call themselves 'rodents' when only in genes and teeth can they call themselves such. But this commission has proven its trustworthiness. Your Comrade Steely knows for a fact that Supreme Commissar of RODEXCOM Pike, our tomcat of evolution, will fulfill his duties to our species without betrayal. I have listed names and associations with these 'Enemies of the Species.' Comrade Steely trusts your judgment, and your decisiveness in this task. Thank you for your service to our species." The Executive RexCom apparatchiki put a period to his speech with their hushed, serious muzzles and thunderous applause.

Later on, the Dzumban who towers over the Big Cheese in private and scurries behind him in public, Comrade Pike inspects a list he has compiled from other lists of known deserters and cowards. I'm sure I appear on several of the lists. As Comrade Chairmouse Fearless, chief of the executive staff in the Rocky Mountain Front, and a Union stalwart, I fight side by side with remarkable rodents, winning across the snow-blanketed mountains out West. The Black Banner of Evolution flies on the burned out frames of the holy places in Salt Lake City, and the liberated human hovels of Boulder. But rank has its privileges.

RexCom. The name that will remain with the souls of rodents for eternity. Like any good marketing scheme, that name, that label, that brand, will represent something, a symbol that stays with the soul, one that can't be forgotten. Pike sits at a table with other lists of accusations and a special stack of files, the personal and private hate stack of the Big Cheese.

Others working for him attend to other sheets, dressed in clean, starched, and pressed dzashes.

Pike picks up a booklet bound with kite string from one of the stacks. "'Co-operative League' . . . what language is this?" he asks his subordinates. A house mouse answers.

"Some Rocky Mountain dialect of Ground Squirrelian, Supreme Commissar."

"Why isn't it Gopherian?"

"They're the same, are they not, Supreme Commissar?"

"And this is from . . ." Pike sniffs out the files, ". . . Fearless. Executive Staff . . . the same Fearless . . . ?"

The mouse smells the booklet and file. "Chairmouse Fearless," he states in conclusion.

The Co-operative Leagues thrive out West at the edge of nature and humanity. The Leagues hold self-sustaining co-operatives that produce their own food, energy, community, and body of laws that help the co-operatives to thrive. Blending Nature's laws and ways with technology pilfered from the humans, the co-operatives provide a way of life that satisfies the soul's needs for shelter, food, comfort, and society. And since each co-operative is independently self-supporting, the leagues can't be broken. Neither dominated nor controlled. That's why I find them so fascinating. But the Tomcat of Evolution smells something else: One of the inner sanctums of leadership in the Union actually exposing himself to that threat.

Pike straightens up, ever so tight and sanctimonious. "The West subverts itself. And . . . it could be planning secession from the Union."

"How do we know this, Supreme Commissar?" asks a porcupine.

"Because it makes sense. And I am in charge," comes Pike's reply.

The Union is one universe among the others in the multi-verse. And this universe, as a living organism, needs a system to inventory and cleanse itself of its unhealthy elements. That is the task of this commission, this commissariat. These Black Caps are the white blood cells of the Union. And a liver is in the works.

*"All the multiverse becomes a mosaic of universes when the personalities of Rodentia gather themselves into the Collective. And each universe dies when ROCOCOLACO purrs at them, 'You are under arrest!'"*

—BUGS CAPPUCCINO, VANGUARD OF NATURE

## Chapter Twelve

# PARALLEL UNIVERSE

L ife's good! I think for me, war brings out a counter-or-gasmic energy. Instead of that orgonic sex and there-fore life energy, war fills me with the death and killing energy. A power in its own right.

Only Dinosaurs have guilty pleasures. I thoroughly enjoy the rush I get from being in the midst of all the shooting and violence that happens in a firefight. I love the hormones pumping through my body when I'm in mortal combat, and thus far, I survived every encounter. War is the natural func-tioning state of Nature. Conflict, strife, getting one over a rival, the constant press upward toward the pinnacle of the pyramid of hierarchy . . . this is the imperative within all organisms and superorganisms that brings us to our very best.

A gentle rain pummels the frozen snow-packed Colorado landscape. The earlier rains froze, turning into a sheet of ice that shrouds the roads and pathways in the late morning of a gray, almost colorless day. Long past my nest time. I want to sleep, but in wartime, that is a luxury not afforded to either me, the supreme commander, nor the other ranks.

This morning, we fly aboard the airborne command post. Along with a combat gaggle of six other rotary-winged warbirds, we airborne rats participate in response to a half-hearted counterattack by the enemy, most of which are irregular forces, militia Dinosaurs, dressed in their civilian clothes, and armed with whatever they can get their paws on. Along Highway 86, running through the smoldering ruins of suburbia, our dead enemies lie piled up in the gutters along the curbs.

"Does it ever get better than this, Cat Claw?" I shriek, over the steady rhythm of the warbird's rotor.

"What?"

"All this." I point my muzzle at the dead strewn across the burning buildings.

"Brother! Comrade! I've seen enough violence in my life," he squeals to me with an air of contempt. Cat Claw is a veteran of the mouse wars last year, and perhaps I touched a nerve he wanted to lie dormant.

"We're going to win this war, brother!" I opine, maybe at this point, more to myself.

A Dinosaur round rips through the body of our cheebah, which shakes me out of my ecstasy. As the other cheebahs bounce around beside us, every rat in the flock looks with myopic eyes for the enemy. BBs hit our bird, shattering the Plexiglas by my face. One piece hits my muzzle, causing a dull pain.

"I see 'em!" comes squawking over the intercom. Our bird drops out of the sky, an aluminum raptor with the heart of a wolverine and the soul of a hummingbird. The cheebah levels out. The command post vibrates with the low-pitched rattle of the main guns.

"Comrade Fearless! Want to smell the dead?" comes the offer over the intercom.

"Negative, Brother Stoner! I need to get to the LZ!" I call over the microphone.

"Yes, Comrade Fearless!"

"I love the smell of dead humanity in the morning, Cat Claw!" I squeak.

I think he mumbles "Original," or something like that.

I conclude, "It smells like . . . evolution!"

I ignore our paw-work outside, only because I bear the responsibility for over four hundred thousand of my siblings. But we're doing well, and I feel happy with our progress against humanity. As long as we stay united, we will win this war. That will be the first and foremost legacy we will give our pups, and all our descendants. Unity.

The RLA holds Denver, Boulder, and Salt Lake City firmly in its paws. Now we press south without letup. North of us, Greeley burns as we scamper through its streets. We've killed hundreds of thousands in the last two weeks. Elsewhere, Fort Myers falls, joined by two thirds of Florida. A stalemate in El Paso leaves those twin cities uninhabitable for the humans, but still comfortable for us. Chee Ka Go's South Side is ours, with multiple rocket batteries aimed north into the city center, and southeast into Indiana. The rat blood spilled has been the great investment of the lives of 1.3 million fighters martyred already. Nothing can go wrong for us, now.

Our cheebah lands. A snub-nosed truck, a clone of a Dinosaur utility vehicle, stops at the landing pad. Hanging out over the sides, RexCom fighters sniff my way. I smell a human in all this RexCom stuff. Phew!

Fear is not a concept I, Fearless, deal with. I don't emote on that level, perhaps. When I sense fear, I attack the stimulus. In the Sheep Pokerian dialectic, flight is the negation of fight, and I always choose the thesis. I smell myself as a true friend of Nature, an equal to any rodent, a resonance of the positive, a faithful and courageous leader at the foundation of power, and a free rat. At least in my soul.

An officer hops out of the truck's cab, sniffs my way, and then scampers up to me. "Comrade Fearless, I presume."

"What do you want?" I, the Rocky Mountain Front commander, squeal with nervous tension. I mean, when was the last time they approached anyone like they really cared?

"I am Comrade Senior Officer Spike Sheeshchikeek, commander of the 9th lishek, 3rd battalion of the . . ."

"Cut the scat, Black Cap. You're RexCom. What do you . . . ?"

"Have no fear, comrade. I come here with glad tidings. Tiding of salvation." The RexCom worker hands a summons to me in a little cardboard message tube. A summons! Obviously, RexCom doesn't know who I am. Despite all their ever-growing database on each of us.

The rain intensifies as the wet and cold me scampers up to the entry of a huge cardboard box covered with a tarp made from black thirty-three–gallon garbage bags. Used. The filthy side takes the stabs of the falling rain as the smooth outer side, now turned inside out, shrouds the interior of the box in darkness and emits that styrene aroma of plastic army men. Just like so many of the RLA meetings in the field. A smell that comforted me throughout my war-fighting service. Until right now.

"Please. Come forward." The voice comes from the darkness. Had this been an RLA tent, I would welcome this opportunity to be a part of such an undertaking. But being a RexCom tent, it has a stinky fart-gas beckoning air about it, coming from the bowels of the Union, ready to move its waste elements.

"State your name and your purpose!" I command.

"There's no need for that here, brother. Please enter so we can squeak muzzle to muzzle."

I put my fur up and lift my hind end in a defensive crouch. "The invitation to squeak about the de-infestation of this neighborhood is a ruse!" I squeal into the darkness.

The voice replies from the darkness, "Comrade. We must not fight each other. If we lose the unity that binds us, the Dinosaurs will call themselves liberators. Please. You have no reason to be afraid. We play an important role together."

Silence, then I venture in. So uncharacteristically tentative, at least for me, I might add. Creeping into the darkness of the tent, I sniff the interior, detecting many bodies, many rats, all Dzumbani. I hear someone scampering behind me. I turn around to face six or so Dzumbani with submachine guns aimed at me, squatting in the doorframe. All of them are bristling up their fur, each of them couldn't have more than four months of this life under their belts. The tarp drops as lights illuminate the interior of the box. A dozen or so RexCom officers in full uniform, complete with black kepi, stand on all fours with their fur bristled and their backs up. I chatter my teeth at them, swishing my tail with hostility. I know damned well what this is. I'm not going down without a fight! I bound into the middle of them, ready to mix it with these Dzumbani bug thorners.

"You are under arrest!" hiss the RexCom rats, bearing their lower teeth.

"Oh, yeah? What for?"

"You dared to degrade and disagree with the Big Cheese!" squeals the highest ranking RexCom officer, under a twelve-inch bust of Steely that stinks of his urine. "And you're a co-operativist!"

So how did my interest in the Co-operative Leagues bite his nut sack? I stop for a minute. The young ones prod me to go before the leading RexCom officer who emerges from the dark shadows.

"And your evidence is . . . ?" I protest to him.

"We are now under the laws of War Collectivism! We don't need evidence!"

The young ones guard me as unsmelled rats the size of cats hop out from who knows where to grab me. I bite back with the courage of a cornered rat. Biting and scratching, we all wrestle, a lopsided rat king of violence. Other guards bring out trash can ties in their muzzles, to tie up my biting advantage with every wrap around my muzzle.

We roll onto a flat object. I get a good sniff, then an image on the flat glass pulls my attention. The photo of the founders! And in the middle, Steely's image has been airbrushed in! As though he founded our Union himself!

I hear a soft thump. I sniff the form dropped in front of me. My whole spirit crumbles as I recognize the pheromone of my beloved Catnip. The RexCom traitors surround her. I whistle at her.

"Silence!" shrieks someone behind me.

A strip of human cloth covers my eyes. I blindly attack that rat fink, bounding across the cardboard box interior with

one jump, right on him. I can't bite him but I can sure scratch
the droppings out of him. But all the RexCom rats subdue me.
Afterward, they all take turns on Catnip, violating her within
my earshot. Then we're separated. They cover me with trash
can plastic, so that the filthy side covers my muzzle. I can't
smell my surroundings, but I know where I'm going. With all
the thrill of the kill I had earlier draining out of me. Step One
complete.


Stripped down. Bathed. Put into a cage with more than a doz-
en others, all of us who just arrived on this side of the thin line
between liberty and repression find a place in the group where
we can size up one another. I establish myself right off the bat
as alpha male. I sniff at the other rodents, find the top rung of
the cage inside and piss three big drops to let them know who
I am. The other rodents move around, then stand up to smell
their new leader of the cage. I try to blank out of my soul what
happened to my soul mate, so I can survive here.

   Night comes. We are all wide awake, regardless of whether
we've been up for nights, which I'm sure some of us have
been. We're all RLA, or like myself, Inner Union members
with military assignments. Agitated by this sudden change in
our social status, tormented by the lack of a good day's sleep,
we feel the tension rising among one another, yet the others
recognize me as their go-to rat for hope. I don't think we'll
grasp the depth of this trauma for a long time. Restlessly, we
mill around the cage, and my cellmates feel out their place in
the caged rats' hierarchy.

   "Siblings! Comrades! Pay attention for a minute," I command my cellmates. All lend me their mousy ears, though
three continue to gnaw on the cell bars. The gnawing, clanging

sound could accompany my short soliloquy. "We're all in this predicament together. And as the supreme commander of the Rocky Mountain Front, I want to take advantage of this . . ."

A RexCom fighter approaches our cage, dressed in clean combat uniform, black band on his left arm, and black kepi with a white stripe on his forehead. "Shee, siblings!" he shrieks, "That's the mad cage! And the little emperor stands to show himself the alpha!" So much for my talk.

Another Dzumban scurries up to our cage. "You're all going to disappear! Flushed out of the body. You are the registered insane. And you! Yes, you! Supreme Commander Fearless! Your real name is the former comrade Meekly. Brother Gentle Meekly, a millwright in Workers' Brigade 952 Rocky Mountain Front. But you bugged on the stove. (That's the Dzumban phrase meaning breaking under pressure and killing everyone within smell range.) Do you know how many of the siblings . . . how many you killed?"

"This is a part of the war against our souls." I hiss back, then add, "Where's your evidence?" The prerecorded sound of rat laughter, with all its whistles and clucks, comes over the squeakers.

"The Union laughs at you, Brother Gentle." The rat scurries away, as though he were never there.

"This is not an insane asylum!" I squeal at my cage mates, feeling the need to be the sane one. "Siblings, listen to me please! Let us figure out what we need here. Don't listen to that voice! Listen to the voice that squeaks, 'We can be sound in our souls in the most mind-numbing experience.'" Most pay attention. I can feel it.

But one of my fellow Shries stands up. "I smell a Dzumban! Phew!" He squeals in fear he'll be the tormented bottom of the cage hierarchy. At the back of the cage, behind the noisy Shrie, a Dzumban with burns and bandages all over his body curls up in a ball. He raises his injured body up, to face the rest of us.

"Brothers. I want to work together with you all," The isolated Dzumban states with sincerity. The others bristle up.

"Stay in your place. We don't need you," hisses a Shrie about as big as the Dzumban. The centuries of bad blood between our two species show in the antipathy of a gesture that comes from intimidation like this. The pack rat stands up slowly, depressed by his predicament.

"Why is it always Shries in the cage, when it's Dzumbani who commit most of the crimes?" asks another Shrie, sending it toward the Dzumban.

Within the cage, the Shries find their own place, pushing the Dzumban to one side. The pack rat sits by himself. The other rats, mostly Shries, but three Dzumbani and another pack rat also, squeeze in, taking some strange comfort in the knowledge that they won't be isolated. At least the Shries feel that.

I step into the situation. "Brother Shries," I inquire, "Please, do you want to become just like the worst of the Dzumbani?"

"Don't give me any of your muzzle, Dzumbani-lover!" one of the Shries chatters at me.

"No," I squeal, "We're all siblings! We Shries, of all rodents, must set the example for a new Earth, free of hate!"

"Oh, I get it, Little Big Rat!" squeaks another of my brothers. "Attic rat from the 'burbs! You're too good for the rest of your kind!"

"Where do you get that cat scat?" I throw at him, disgusted by his ignorance. The bottom feeder. "I don't have anything to prove to you!"

The first Shrie lunges for my hinder parts—his attempt to unseat me as the new leader. If we knew each other, and this was all in fun, we would bite each other's necks and wrestle around. I mean, Catnip and I would do it to get each other in the mood for a little ratty sexing, but when we rats aim for the ass, it's serious!

I jump out of his way, and in midair, I pull myself around to land on his back. We both land in the bare metal floor. I bounce on him, grabbing his rump in my teeth. The other Shrie squeals at the others, "Tell him what he is! Rat fink!" He squeals that most insulting slur any rat can throw at another, trying to get the whole group to join in. But as the first submits to me, he crawls away from the silent others. I bite Number Two's ass, to nail my point down, and peace returns to the cage.

After only Nature knows how long, a RexCom house mouse scurries up to the door of the cage. He stands there, playing with the door, dressed in a clean, pressed dark green dress uniform with blue trousers and boots made from black canvas and rubber. I sniff out this well-dressed mouse, sizing him up.

"Would you be the one in charge?" I ask.

The well-dressed mouse wiggles his muzzle my way and feels me out with his whiskers. Then he stands up. "Listen up! The following will step out of the cage when the door opens. Numbers Shay Chee-Chee 3996, 3997, 3899, and Tee, that's Tee, Chec-Chee 8702."

The order blares on the squeakers, hanging above and behind the mouse. "Senior Commander Brie Squeequeehok! Bring the third swarm."

A dozen RexCom fighters scamper out to the door. The well-dressed mouse opens the door as other fighters swarm around the cage, pointing assault rifles the size of golf pencils at the condemned. The ones called out perk their ears toward the open door, then scurry away with the fighters, not resisting. Ever so compliant. This is what concerns me the most.

Chapter Thirteen

# STEP TWO

*A*cross the Rodentian Military/Industrial Complex, the mi-
*crophone becomes the most important weapon of all. And it's
aimed at us, down to every cell in our cottage industry body.
Comrade Steely's bionic ears, as we call them. As much a symbol of
our Union as every statue, bust, portrait, or poster of our elder statesrat
(along with the stink of his urine), the microphone hides in the shadows.
A poster with one rat ear aimed at the viewer says it all with its caption,
"The Big Cheese Hears All!"*

*Accompanying the microphone, the squeaker of the PA system
chirps out tales of treachery by a mythical cabal of Shries. The larynx
of our Union's body. Any of the Shries could be a part of this. They,
who eat Dzumbani babies, poison wells, and plot seditious blood feasts
against all others, weasel into the corridors of power with their feel-good
pseudo-philosophy of personal sovereignty and enfranchisement in gover-
nance. A thirteen hundred–page codex bearing the title* Protocols of
the Old Ones of Shriedaygahbuyaniyaschikita, that Mythical

Motherland of the Shries *pops up throughout the Union rumor mills, though no one has actually seen a copy of this opus. Maybe it doesn't even exist.*

*And in the internet cafes and theaters across the Union, our siblings gather around the monitors to watch the trials of the growing number of traitors who work their iniquities against the Big Cheese. My name popped up frequently as a conspirator. No evidence will be required in the court of public opinion.*

I have no idea of where I am, or what time it is. All I have is the here and now. Brie Squeequeehok's Dzumbani put a black hood over my head, then bind me up in metal electrical wires and plastic twist ties. They drop me onto what feels like a cage with a miserable metal wire floor. No shredded paper to rest on. No chlorophyll-rich wood shavings to absorb the stink of our rotting droppings. All I see is black. But I smell the fear of maybe hundreds of siblings. It's so strong, the hood can't filter it out.

They drag me from cage to cage, cold concrete floor to metal drain cover, then into another cage. The softest material they ever drop me onto is something wooden, maybe a liberated workbench. It smells like a machine shop, which for me is quite comforting.

I sense the presence of several hostile rodents. One of them scurries like a gerbil. They stay in my space, silent, except for the sound of their gnawing teeth on the wires of this cage. Silence. More deafening than being screamed at, hearing bells and alarms blare, or any other auditory stimulus. Over time, the silence and isolation invite inner voices to speak their perspective of truth.

"You can't save the Union, Little Boot," comes a voice from within. I breathe in slowly through my nostrils, out with more force, to build a rhythm that will energize me.

"I couldn't save anyone I love!" I say to myself. Then I change my tune. "Focus on the moment. Smell the pleasing aroma of a babbling brook," I continue, counteracting the negativity within.

My thought-life stops as a memory of my family goes through my mind. Buttercup peeps out to me over the babble of that brook where I smelled her last. And that's what sticks in my soul! Her desperate peep, "Fearless! Fearless! Come get me! Here I am! Where are you?"

"Not Buttercup . . . not Catnip . . . not our Union . . . we're thorned!" comes a voice. I don't know if it came from within, or what.

"Traitor Meekly. Please tell the truth," comes a voice from what sounds like one of the gerbils. But at this point, I'm not so sure. At the sound of that voice, shock waves roll across my body from within.

"Traitor Meekly, why didn't you kill the Dinosaur Lady when you had the chance?" comes the voice of Brie Squeequeehok.

"Dinosaur lover!" comes another voice.

"You lick the cat's asshole and call it symbiosis!" exclaims a Dzumban voice.

"Do you lick Dzumban thorn as well?" another Dzumban shrieks in my ear.

"Sheep Pokerite!" squeaks the voice of a house mouse, with his mousy arrogance.

"Sheep Pokerite!" all the rodents squeal at me, in several different accents.

Then silence, again. After a while, I hear the patter of scurrying, leaving my side, moving through what must be the open door to the cage. And again, I'm alone with my thoughts.

Directly from the capstone comes a calling, the Four-Fold Path of Enlightenment, offered to all of us rodents. We don't choose the calling. It chooses us. And we receive that calling at the First Fold when they hiss at us, "You are under arrest!"

The Second Fold reveals itself through interrogation, when we expose our faulty belief systems, then prepare ourselves for the right soulscape that only acknowledges the Steelian *weltschau*.

But I want my own personal sovereignty. And I love the Union. I thank Nature each and every evening when I get out of the nest that I was born a rodent. And you know, I'm so glad I'm a rat! And we roof rats are no less than any other! I'm not choosing Steely. I'm not the soul-sick one. No one rodent represents our great taxonomic order. Not even Steely, that condescending tail hole.

If ever a rat represented the finest in Nature, it was . . . I'll squeak out her name at the top of my scarred lungs! My special someone! Catnip will always be the girl rat of my ratty rat dreams. Looks don't mean droppings! But a girl rat's aroma can tell you a lot about her. What neighborhood she's from. Whether she values herself. If she's conniving or on the level. Catnip's aroma exudes humility. Fearlessness. Honesty. She's smells better than a thousand pounds of brussels sprouts cooked into cornbread.

After stealing a half hour of sleep, I wake up on the wooden bench and find I'm more than alone. I sense that physical separation. I'm good company when I'm alone but better with my other half, the female side of our street. Torn from me and . . . I can't focus on all that now.

I reach out for her across the astral plane. Someone's there, reaching back to me. And Catnip isn't the only one. I sense in my heart our beloved All Rodents Evolutionary Union beckoning me to remember her. I won't give up on the Union, any more than I will give up on Nature herself, or my family, who embraced Catnip, because they know we're all family now. Also, that mystery rat who goes by Cappuccino, because I still have a hope of our contending species finding equality together. That's it! Together, just different.

The electrical shocks are no worse than the hot water they dumped on me. Yet I sense restraint in the procedure. I'm sure the electrodes they place on my forehead or groin come from some liberated hardware store, where now RexCom manufactures all the devices for interrogation. The feistiness I relied on throughout my life passes out of my spirit with each sleepless night.

The Black Caps undo my bonds. I sniff the air, and instinctively wiggle my whiskers to get a sense of my surroundings. A Black Cap bites me for doing so. All nine assigned to me gather around my prostrate form. The head guard takes his place at my head.

"On the count of three! *Rhee, Chikchik, Taleka . . . ,*" he commands. They lift me off the table, onto a four-castor dolly made of wood, gathering around me afterward. "Let's go."

They push the dolly with their muzzles or their paws as the head guard and two others pull with cord in their jaws. I can still sniff the air, and I smell old mold growing on the baseboards. The tile walls float past us as the click-click-click rhythm of the castors provides the only soundtrack. At another room, the nine turn toward the open door. I feel the turn, gently breathing, smelling my surroundings, which still stinks of mold, water damage, and sorrow. Then the aroma of fresh flowers fights with the depressing stink.

"Watch your tails," commands the head guard.

The group shifts forward. A steady roll to a microwave oven, where again, the dolly shifts, now to the left, and I move with the shift. The dolly stops in front of the microwave's open door.

Off comes the blindfold. After taking two-thirds of an eternity to adjust, my beady eyes can see the surroundings. To my right, the microwave oven. To my left, a Shrie in bad shape, and a gerbil. The nine pick up one side of the dolly with their teeth. I roll off onto the tile, then, in my dizzy state from an eternity of abuse and sleep deprivation, try to stand on all fours.

"Stand at attention, you filthy dung beetle!" squeals the head guard. The well-dressed officer from before scurries up to the microwave with a clipboard in his mouth. A group of rodents, maybe fifty or sixty in all, scampers out of the surroundings, taking their places around the microwave. The crew who brought me in now grab me with their teeth and pull me to sit with the other two. The head guard stops them. "He can stay."

When everybody is ready, the well-dressed officer stands in front of the microwave oven's door. He pulls a clipboard out of his mouth with his paws and reads the contents.

"Comrades! Siblings! By authority of the War Collectivism Central Committee, empowered by the Will of the Species, we, the Ninth Regiment of the 613th Corrective Labor Division of the All Rodents Extraordinary Commission, hereby fulfill the execution of the sentence upon the following: Gerdzik Chukchukchuk! You were sentenced to die for the charges of aiding and abetting the enemy, desertion, raping a baby bunny, and pissing on a bust of . . . the Big Cheese . . ." Apart from myself and the two other condemned rodents, all bow toward a bust of Steely sitting on the microwave, wreathed with fresh flowers.

"Now, we will fulfill that sentence. The rest of you . . . listen!"

A stethoscope goes up to the side of the oven. A video camera created from a smartphone goes to the window. A fifty-one-inch monitor stands behind the oven. The view from the camera lights up the screen, with The Big Cheese's bust standing in front of it.

As he struggles to get loose, the guards drag the gerbil into the oven. "Thump" goes the door as it closes.

"Executioner, perform your duty!" squeals the well-dressed officer.

A guard presses the "start" switch. The gerbil moves around, then shakes violently. On the screen, the image looms over the bust of the Big Cheese as the gerbil explodes, spraying his fur and flesh on the oven's window. And with the ring of a bell, the light in the oven goes out.

The Shrie goes into the oven after his sentence is read. He cooks on screen after less than a minute of microwave power. Guards pull me into the flesh-strewn oven interior. Before the door closes, the well-dressed officer points his Dzumban muzzle at me and reads the sentence as I sit helplessly in the oven.

"By authority of the War Collectivism Central Committee, empowered by the Will of the Species, we, the Ninth Regiment of the 613th Corrective Labor Division of the All Rodents Extraordinary Commission, hereby fulfill the execution of the sentence upon the following: Traitor Gentle Meekly! By a tribunal that rightly hides itself, you have been found guilty of the following charges . . . Cowardliness in the face of the enemy! Desertion! And belittling the Big Cheese behind his back! Executioner! Perform your duty!"

The door closes. A shroud falls over the window . . .

## Chapter Fourteen

# THEATER OF THE ABSURD

Several nights later, the door opens. I feel hot spots on my skin and sores on my body as I lie on the oven's hard, putrid floor. Guards pull me out and dump me on another dolly. Down we go through the tiled walls of the hallway, accompanied by the castors' click-click-click.

While waiting for the microwave to cook me, I heard a voice chirp from the ventilation grate in the oven repeating, "Don't quit. Surrender!" Then I heard the confessions of Nature knows how many rodents, saying the same confession, over and over, ". . . Please, while my soul stands clean, and it stands *unsullied* (what a sissy word!) by humanistic influence, kill me now, confessing only my undying love for our glorious leader, the Big Cheese." They must be actors and actresses reading this cat scat!

Anyway, the guards drop me off in a psychiatrist's office. They lift the dolly and I drop off, right in front of the psychiatrist, who stinks of alcohol. He vibrates like he suffers with some palsy. Behind him stands a poster with a human child's hand taking an old human's hand into its own. Splashed over it in Ratsqueak letters is the imperative, "Don't quit. Surrender." Across from it, behind a row of improvised desks sits a bust of the Big Cheese.

"Greetings, Traitor Meekly. How are we today?" the *SICK*-iatrist slurs at me. I move slowly on the floor, away from the not-so-good doctor. One of the guards pulls off the duct tape over my muzzle.

"Squeak!" commands the guard. I sniff the air.

"I don't know about me. But you smell like Dinosaur scat." I chirp with hostility.

The guards bite me on the ass, avoiding the black tag on my tail.

"Traitor Meekly . . . you pissed li'l mouse . . . You need a bath. So why don't you smell yourself, you puke," replies the doctor.

I hit back with, "It's your lies and the Big Cheese that stink."

"Execute him!" squeals the head guard. He points his service revolver at me, then remembers the black tag. "On second thought, shoulder arms!"

"Senior fighter," squeaks the Doctor. "I can handle . . . more than handle a soused mouse like him . . . soused mouse . . . I think the good doctor will prescribe 'imself another gram of my soul mediation . . . medication . . . but firs' . . . I declare the souse mouse of the house fully . . . capable . . . of standing trial for all the crimes against Nature. Traitor Gentle Meekly . . . please, pay attention."

"You're the traitor. All of you!" I throw at him because he's a part of a great finky treason to our Union.

"Why do you say that, little Meekly?" he asks, to reinforce my subordinate place in this hierarchy.

I hit him with, "Use my real name, fink!"

"Oh . . . tay, fink the mink it is . . . Meekly mink the fink. Does that . . . that . . . fit the bill for you, little brother?"

"I ain't your little brother. I am the supreme commander and executive commissar of the Rocky Mountain Front." I won't back down to this head game.

"My, minky . . . inky, fearless finky. The spirits are about to squeak!"

"My name is Fearless! Comrade Supreme Officer Fearless. Chairmouse of the Ninth International!"

The doctor pauses for a moment. He enters into deep thought as he gnaws on a piece of wood taken from a human desk. Then he slurs in a flat, patronizing, and emotionally detached squeak. "Well, what a powerful fantasy wife you have . . . life . . . you . . . have."

I bite him with, "Who are you working for, you pissed slave?"

"Lower your voice!" shrieks the doctor.

"No!"

Again, that Nature-damned patronization, "You are a naughty pup now, aren't you?"

I'm hissing pissed now, "And you haven't spent a day in combat! So close the faucet on your diarrhea!"

"Do I have to spend time in combat to prove my place over you?'"

"This isn't my place."

"It is now, little brother." The guards scurry over and put a strip of fresh, gray duct tape around my muzzle. "Brother Meekly," he glares in parting, "Don't quit. Surrender."

A bottle with a thin streak of emerald-green algae kept alive in its water hangs on my cage, shaking from my attempt to get more hydration. Above me, a white Dzumban, collaborator with the Dinosaur Scientific Community, pisses drops of pee down on me.

"Hey, white meat! Quit pissing on me!" I command to the rat fink.

White meat shows his true nature with, "Thorn yourself, Shrie. Seems like you forgot your place!"

"Where were you, tail hole, when we liberated Boulder? In a cage in a human laboratory!" I throw at him.

White meat takes a dump, which hits me in the face. Then he looks down with his piss-poor pinkeye vision. "Now, you know your place, Jeemsh."

I hit him back with, "Pup thornin' snowflake!"

RexCom guards scurry in, in front of an entourage of officers and three doctors in white lab coats grazing the floor. They stop at the cage door below mine, where there are some mice nestled together in a corner. I always pooped in the other corner, so as not to condescend them.

Across from the cages, a monitor liberated from an electronics shop blares the trials of spies and traitors. Threats to the species. And who shows up on the screen? Comrade Spunky Kcherkckertecherkh, the Gopherian brother from the northern Rockies who lived near a body of water named Lake Louis. Dozens of months ago, he happened to find a Dinosaur with a photo apparatus pointing at him. That photo was the best picture ever taken of him. It is now the worst. It appears big on the monitor, with Spunky defined well, and two humans to the right, his left, behind him. They scoffed at him, for the sincerity and proud visage he exudes in his portrait. From the screen, he stands up to defend himself.

"And I'm not humbling myself! I see in myself a Golden-mantled ground squirrel. And I'm proud of it! I bear in myself a special love for my species, just as I love our order, our sacred cause, and Nature's call. And my trial follows the infomercial!" I hope this isn't the last time I ever see him. Spunky and I have no business in a cage. But Grand Mother Nature knows who is Hers.

After that appearance and those shameful and false accusations against Spunky, the monitor shows a cartoon liberated from the Dinosaurs. A siwi wabbit in a striped swimsuit runs out of a hole along a sand dune. In bloody terror, he hysterically shrieks in the Dinosaur tongue, "Whoo! Hoo! My Yiami Beach at last!" Then our brave and fearless Rodents Liberation Army/Navy lands under fire on the beach to liberate Collins Park in My Yiami, Florida. Over thirty pirated ships rebuilt to conduct amphibious operations hits the beach. On board other Dinosaur freighters turned warships, cargo containers launch the remaining cruise missiles left over from Night One. Still other containers point 122mm and 130mm multiple rocket launchers at downtown My Yiami Beach. In salvos and ripples they fill the air with smoke and the aroma of burning cordite, fireworks against humanity. Later, 8x8 amphibious ATVs, landing with dozens of our marine infantry onboard, roll onto the beach up to the burning buildings. Over the inland waterways, our piston-driven aircraft fly over the hovels and swimming pools of the islands, attacking yachts and suburban-looking neighborhoods.

A webcam records a firefight in My Yiami. The Great Sacred War for Evolution will be the last war humanity experiences, and the first one watched by both sides on smartphones. Nights before, My Yiami was invaded by our glorious RLA from the liberated Everglades, heading east to meet the

siblings on the beach. The RLA made it as far as the big air-
field, which provides us with a huge air power base that we
can use to dominate both the petroleum-saturated Gulf and
the Caribbean, once we take it. But didn't we already liberate
My Yiami?


The operating theater is a place for surgery of the souls of
the siblings who fall into error. Here is where the patients
will be brought to a place of reasonability, where they can
admit their faults in this purest of "criticism/self-criticism"
sessions. In its purest form, the patients listen to criticism,
then they must criticize themselves. For the Union is infallible, as is its most noble member, the Big Cheese. All is
accomplished within accordance of Nature's approval. So
squeaks the AREU.

Free from my duct tape bonds, I crawl through a hole
about an inch wide, then scamper onto the inner floor, trying
to establish my location. I look up and can barely make out
what appears to be over thirty uniformed rodents of RexCom
and the Union behind a wall of light, observing me. On the
opposite side of the stage, four big Dzumbani scurry out into
the light bathing the stage floor. They sniff the air in my direction, with complete hubris.

"I smell a human. Phew!" reports the biggest one.

"I say, stinks like a treasonous rat fink. Open the thornin'
window, would yah?" adds another.

"Stinks like a Jeemsh," the smallest of the four squeaks.

"I've been thorning your woman, Dzumie!" I offer, as a
conversation opener. Perhaps too much information for the
species-ist bigot.

"And what makes you think I even like girls, Jeemsh?" he counters.

I hit him with, "Yeah, your squeak makes you sound as queer as a prison gerbil."

The four Dzumbani jump on me. All five of us roll around on the floor, scratching, biting each other, shrieking.

"Traitor Meekly! Is it true you have cat syphilis?" queries the familiar voice of a uniformed senior AREU apparatchik.

"At ease, you dirty Dinosaurs!" commands the senior fighter to the four, who all move away from me in terror. Sitting alone in a cage made me grow a new ball sac. I remain defiant, unbroken. I sniff the air in the direction of the voice.

"Is that you, Cat Claw?" I ask, wondering if my assistant was what I suspected all along.

"Be still, you thorned bug!" shrieks the sergeant of arms, a twenty-inch-long muskrat who stinks like a mink.

"No, let him ask," replies the apparatchik.

"I was being watched the whole time, wasn't I, Cat Claw?"

The reply comes, "You were being listened to. And smelled." But something doesn't add up. I think maybe the voice comes from a machine.

"And what is it you want?" I ask.

"We just want a clean, happy Earth. Nothing more." His reply sounds so hypocritical.

"But I'm not a dust speck!"

"Thorn him!" comes the command from this figure I once trusted with my life.

The four attack me again. More rat fighting, balled up in rodent hostility. Then I slip through the ball of fur and tails, and bite one in the ass. Then another, and the third. The four scamper to the holes, with the biggest going to the wrong one, the small one I came out of. In the hole, the fourth Dzumban gets stuck. I catch up to him, then coming up from behind I grab his tail, pull it up with my teeth, and mock hump the bigot to establish my dominance.

"Want some kitty syph, tail hole?" I cry, to the whole congregation of hate masquerading as love.

Our Union, the AREU, is my greatest affection; its success, my great desire. My whole life is committed to its victory and healing of the Earth. And this is how I'm treated. But still, there is one rat that I can trust. But she is here being raped and prostituted out by these true traitors and seditionists, rat finks in the truest meaning of the slur, these who squeak of Nature, yet stink of humanity.

Back in our cages, a Dzumban gnaws on our adjoining cage bars. Having just returned from kicking tail four at a time, this Dzumban means nothing to me. But I sure want to know where our unity went, especially since unity is our first legacy to our descendants. I scamper to the cage wires and brush my body against this rat.

"Lay off the cage! My chew wire," I shriek.

The other rat slinks away in sorrow and submission. "Sorry. I didn't know."

I stop, allowing my rat testosterone to moderate, then I chirp at the rat in a reconciliatory voice.

"Maybe I overreacted. You need a bar to gnaw on."

"Yes. I do."

"Take that other end."

The two of us spend three nights next to each other, never having another angry interaction.

More rats slowly scurry in, some resigned to whatever will come, most just confused. The most confused and lost are the RexCom officers purged from the Union. One scurries into the cage behind me.

"*Khlee Rotyetska!*" jeers a house mouse at the ex-Black Cap from a few cages down. "For Rodentia!" in House Mousian. "That's Urban, Eastern House Mousian!" squeaks the mousy brother.

The other inmates sniff the air around Black Cap. "So are we all traitors now, Comrade Black Cap?" squeaks the mouse. Black Cap turns to me, as if I had any empathy for this fink.

"Brother, could you help me out?"

I sniff the air in this new neighbor's cage. "I can tell by your stink that you're a Dzumban."

"But, comrade, what does that matter?" he responds.

"Ha! You hate us because our ears and thorns are bigger than yours. By millimeters!"

"But I am innocent! I am faithful! I . . . it had to be someone else . . . someone out to get me."

"It always is, brother," offers the Dzumban who made peace with me.

"And what were you charged with?" I ask.

"Why should I answer to you now?" the ex-RexCom Dzumban snaps back at me.

"Relax, brother. We're all in this together," I add.

"Listen to him, comrade," requests my new Dzumban friend next door.

Black Cap shrinks up into a corner, sniffing the bars for a clean chew. "I don't know. I was serving in the 13th RexCom Division. I led a crew of sappers that were . . . species secret!"

The mouse squeaks his mind again. "Comrade Black Cap! Are they purging the RexCom now?"

"That's stupid!"

"Or is it?" replies the mouse.

"It's easy for you to squeak, mouse! You're safe behind bars!" Black Cap counters, trying to keep the faith.

"I'd rather be in my AgitProp APC," squeaks the mouse. "The one with the loud squeakers! The ones we scream with at the Dinosaurs at night, when we're wide awake and they can't sleep! 'Dirty Dinosaurs! You die tonight, Dinosaurs! We come and skin your cats!'"

"You never spent a night in a fire fight!" Black Cap states.

The mouse dodges the question, "Have you?"

"Yes."

"How much have you seen?"

"More than you."

The mouse won't be out done by a mere rat. "I've killed two cats and a Dinosaur boy, bug thorner! And I may have no more time, so killing a rat would be sweet pleasure before I die!" And with that the mouse tells the truth. The whole truth.


One night, I get bundled up with duct tape and thrown into a black van. I could see that much as they taped my eyes closed. After bouncing around in the dark, I feel the cold stainless steel edge of a pair of medical scissors cutting me loose. I could sense I was airborne for a long time. The only real contact I had with anyone else came when someone hydrated my body, giving me water from a tube pushed through the duct tape into my mouth. When I can see again, I find myself in a poorly lit room with huge Dinosaur toilets and piss pots on the walls, through which the Dinosaurs wasted so much fresh drinking water.

"Here is your wardrobe," whistles a gopher dressed in a white lab coat. At my feet sits tonight's duty uniform: a clean and pressed dzash with trousers, and a new pair of rubber and canvas boots we teasingly named "Chucky Tees." The lack of nutrition and steady movement has left me with almost no physical power to employ. Or resist.

"Put on the uniform, slacker!" the gopher chirps with rancor, whistling out in his western Gopherian accent. That's when I eye the rodent and sniff him out. The gopher gets into my muzzle. He whistles at me, "Don't you eyeball me!"

"You're a treasonous fink!" I hiss through all my deprivation.

"Just put them on, or else . . . we'll put them on for you. Do I make myself perfectly clear?"

"Who can understand you with that gopher whistle?" I throw at him. Then I turn to my new wardrobe. The gopher scampers off. When he returns, nine huge African hooded rats accompany him. All scurry in, to find me fully clothed and in my right, free mind.

"Traitor Gentle Meekly! You are to come with us. Follow us, please!" commands the biggest one.

I yield, "As you wish, comrade."

"You are no longer a comrade," squeaks the smallest and most vicious-smelling of the nine.

The entourage directs me into a soundstage with twelve other accused rodents dressed in the finest attire. I notice our dzashes lack pockets. A symbol of our new status. We take our places at a table, with each of us having a cardboard name-plate sitting in front of us. After time passes, a bank of lights clicks on, burning its glare into our beady black eyes. Beyond the glare, the light of a video camera comes on, then several others join it.

"Comrades! Siblings! Before you sit the enemies of the species! Traitors! Spies for Argentina and the weasels! Slackers and cowards! And most antinatural of all . . . the weird!"

A tribunal of thirteen rodents, about half Dzumbani, but also two house mice, and the token Shrie sit with their fur bristling up on their backs. The one with the most brass on his uniform, an ugly fox squirrel with black mousy fur, recites from a list on a piece of paper taken from a liberated notebook. He ends it by introducing the star of the show trial.

"Comrade Chief Prosecutor Dzinka Dzeebeediyah will now take his place!" whistles the fox squirrel.

Out of a curtain to the left, stage right, the prosecutor enters with a cardboard tube in his jaws. The PA system blares out a beautiful ditty about our great Rodentian order. The thirteen join in singing the song as the prosecutor stands in the light.

"Comrades," Dzinka purrs, the sound of his voice reverberating through the court room. "We come into this beautiful world as the most fortunate of all animals. Don't you feel grateful tonight to be a rodent?" The thirteen whistle in excitement. We, the other thirteen, remain silent.

The fox squirrel clucks through his microphone, "Traitor Meekly! Squat and be counted!"

Two Dzumbani guards nip at me. I pull myself up slowly.

Dzinka opens his case against me, "Comrades! Siblings! I beg you to share with me! Does the Shrie squatting before you smell like he . . . excuse me, Traitor Meekly, you are a boy rat, aren't you?"

"Answer him 'yes' or 'no,' you Nature-hating stinkbug!" squeals the fox squirrel.

"Comrade Dzinka . . ." I answer, then wince when Dzinka rips into me.

"Don't you call me 'comrade!' Ever!" the former comrade Dzinka chatters, in that chatter all of we rats know well. The one that signals a violent fight is brewing. He relaxes, but just a little, then asks, "Yes or no!"

"Boy rat with a pink thorn that can paint a white rabbit green with envy!" I reply.

"That should be an instant death sentence right there!" interjects the fox squirrel.

The thirteen erupt with, "To the Microwave! Nuke 'im! Nuke 'im! Nuke 'im!" Across our great Rodentia, this phrase flashes in white Rodentian letters. Usually, if possible, the scent of cat pee goes with it. To the good citizens of our Union, I must die. And I smell like American beer.

Dzinka takes the focus of attention back. "Traitor Meekly! It seems you stated on your duty report dated Night Fifteen, 'No live enemy engaged in the ruins.' That's what you put down? Yes or no?"

"And none of your muzzle!" squeals the fox squirrel.

"Yes," I answer.

"But a Dinosaur with a baby was smelled in the ruins by a unit of RexCom combatants. It must have been a mother Dinosaur because we smelled disposable diaper in the air. So you lied on your report?" I refuse to answer the accusation and wonder if the Dinosaur mother made it to safety.

"Answer the chief prosecutor!" the thirteen command.

"You lie like pig, don't you, Meekly?" Dzinka throws at me. "Maybe you're a human-lover. Maybe . . . ," Dzinka paces in front of me in full view of the cameras, ". . . You keep a pet kitten hidden in your former command post!" In my mind, the image of a kitty flashes on the screen with letters spelling out, "Fearless's Scaredy Cat!"

Dzinka paces a little more, gnaws on the furniture, and then sniffs at me, "Meekly? Is this any way to show your gratitude to our beloved Comrade Steely Dzugash Veeley?"

"I owe Steely nothing!" I slur, inviting a gasping whistle to flow out of the muzzle of every rodent in the room.

"Selfishness!" The prosecutor shrieks, "Self-centeredness! Those, it appears, are the roots of your problem!" Dzinka squats in front of me. He thoughtfully comments, "Each of we members of the All Rodents Evolutionary Union, in fact every one of we rodents, has the burden of self-expression lifted from us, thanks to our glorious leader . . ." Once again, the bow to the bust of the Big Cheese, then he continues, "But not from this traitor before me! He'd rather think for himself!" Another gasp flows from the thirteen. "When are you ever going to grow the thorn up?"

After a lot of squawking and squealing about Nature knows what, and the justice system of the Union's presentation of false evidence, the lights dim. Never is an opportunity given to express another disagreement or dissent. We all know we're guilty as charged, even if we aren't. After final pronouncements of our guilt, we thirteen slowly scurry away into oblivion, escorted out after the light returns to blare on us. That torturing light is the glory of our deaths to the Union.

"Only through great suffering will the damned experience their psychic changes. To have their souls saved from anti-Steelian expression and Dinosaurian humanism's insanity, great soul quakes within will be needed. The Union's soul must go through a psychic change as well. In our Union's collective thought-life—its passion and collective will—we must conform to the standard set by Comrade Steely," squeaks the mousy new supreme doctrinarian, Limburger Squeeteet. "But this can only come through its relationship with Nature and Her true husband, the Divine Reality. These are our parents, our holy family. This holy family must lead and dictate."

I hear Limburger lecture to us across the PA system. Of course, there's no way of arguing with him. The debate is over.

Steely is not the voice of Nature any more than any other rodent. Since I'm already damned as a traitor and a spy for Argentina (and I'm no wuss or slacker, dammit!), I'll squeak it! The soul of the All Rodents Evolutionary Union heads for failure against humanity with this new meme, Steely Dzugash Veeley. Oh, divine family! Nature, our holy Grand Mother! Above all, you, great divine reality! Please, draw us to the meme you would have for us!


After more duct tape, flying, and being pulled through unseen locations stinking of mold and humanity, I rest untaped in a cell made from bricks and mortar, the aroma of fresh concrete still in the air. I smell the new guards as they sniff their way down the halls. These young ones in RexCom uniforms, twenty-week-olds with no respect for their fellows, take the dominant role over us, the older, more experienced rodents. Yet I feel compassion for them, though they sure don't for me. They seem like they lack a family. Strong father and mother figures. And they are so incredibly ignorant. They're not stupid, but they have no grasp of consequences.

The sound of scurrying arrives at the entrance of the cell. Metal clinks and clanks. The door swings open. In scampers young RexCom fighters and Evolutionary Youths. An Officer of the Extraordinary Commission Central Committee scurries in with a paper list in his jaws. Standing up on his back legs, he takes the list in his weak little T. rex arms and reads with an authoritative, mousy voice.

"Attention! Attention! Your attention, please. The following will follow us out. Chee Stinker Dzushchish! Ugly Tail Hole Kishkaghebrahzheedahhee! Annette!"

"No girl rats in here, comrade!"

"Shut up! Don't ever interrupt an officer of the All Rodents Extraordinary Commission! Now . . . Annette? Annette? Sewer Raider! Gentle Meekly . . . !"

The theater sits with its stage bathed in light. That's the place where I insulted the Dzumbani and smelled who I think might be Cat Claw. Observers sit behind the glare, watching me, as Dinosaur doctors would do more than a century ago in a university surgical theater. Not unlike the show (and squeak nothing) trial.

I slowly scurry through the same door I came out of before. Only this time, it smells like I am alone. Maybe.

"Why are you here, Traitor Meekly?" squeaks a voice from behind the glare.

"My name is Fearless! Comrade Chairmouse of the Ninth International Fearless! Address me as that!" I hiss out, with every bit of reserve and resolve I have left in me. If I die, nuked in the microwave for Steely's cowardice, at least I won't break.

"Our clinical psychiatrist says you have delusions of grandeur," comes a different voice, sounding feminine and Marmotian.

"That soused moused rat is crazy," I stab back.

The first voice parries with, "And, of course. You are the last sane rat on Earth."

I know my soul is clean. "There's more of us, you rat finky traitor!" I punch out with a weakening verbal *sai ken*.

"But you're all alone. You don't even know your name," comes his block, with that sparrow-thorning, patronizing chirp. I sniff around for something to gnaw on.

"Why are you here, Meekly?" comes a familiar voice, Shrie, feminine, earthy, and sensual. But its resonance is now so dissonant. I freeze, paying close attention to my surroundings.

"You brought me here," I answer.

That patronizing first voice kicks me with, "You're in this facility to heal that soul sickness within you. You don't even know the seriousness of your condition."

I defy them with, "The only thing soul-sick is our Union. Our order! What have you done with our species?"

A door opens from the other side of the stage. I sniff the air and get the most horrendous visceral horror flowing through my whole being, like a current of black electricity. My heart melts. Scurrying out to meet me, the girly Shrie with the most recognizable silhouette takes center stage. I scurry to her, smelling the aroma on her fur as she smells mine. Blended in with her delicious fragrance is the sickening stink of cat pee. When we separate, a thick glass panel comes crashing down between us with a thump so full of bass that we feel the sound more than hear it. We both paw the glass, trying to confirm who we smelled is who we think it is.

Then down the tops of the stage, a Dinosaur woman, wearing nothing but a dog collar as punishment for her failures, steps over into my space. On the other side, a Dinosaur man steps in with the same kind of collar apparatus on his neck. I stand up to get a good whiff of what's in my territory. The female Dinosaur stinks of cat pee and human feces,

sending the most morbid disgust through every vibration in
my soul and body. She attacks me with human poop as Dinosaur music vibrates my space. And it's that bubblegum scum
noise from the SICK-sties, as the enemy calls it. I dodge,
bite, squeal, and remain in downward dog pose with my fur
puffed out, coming muzzle to muzzle with a fear I never
knew I had . . . Dinosaur nudity. And on the other side of
the glass, my better half finds a hidden fear within herself,
phallophobia: fear and loathing of the Dinosaur penis. The
thorn for her is a joy. At least mine was. But this is a Dinosaurian weapon.

The bleeding, rat-bit woman finally gets me in her freshly
battle-scarred hands. She gazes at me in a somnambulistic
stare of . . . No! Wait a second! My Nature! The Dinosaur
is drawing me up to her lady parts! I'm going in through the
gates of her innermost hell!

"Do it to Catnip!" roars out of my muzzle, as though I
were an angry cannon firing a shot.

"What's that, Meekly?" comes a voice from the panel of
faithful Steelyists.

"Fearless! My name is Fearless!" I shriek in terror.

Another voice comes to me, "We're holding the beast
back. Like to get anything off your chest?"

"Do it to Catnip! Do it to Catnip! Squee!" I plead.

"To Catnip? Feed Catnip to the Dinosaur's perversity?"
comes a reply. I can't believe I squeaked that. But I did.

Over the sound system, the sound of Catnip squeaking reverberates, a dark, peepy shriek of betrayal. "Do it to Fearless!
He's the soul-criminal! He's *a spy for Argentina*!"

"Feed Catnip to the guard minks!" I shriek like a mad
mouse on crystal methamphetamine.

"As you wish, Brother Fearless . . ."

Across our great order, the order of Rodentia, we have information technology liberated from the dirty humans, who now squat in the squalor of their collapsed western civilization, burning with starvation and anarchy. Our sound systems keep us up to date. And our telescreens, created from liberated phones and beautiful sixty-five-inch screens, (and even bigger, carried around on trailers!), all in unison play the latest war news, the never-ending production reports, commodities owned by the Union, and the confessions of the enemies within.

I never quit. But I surrender. My contrition fills the million or so screens across the Union with a gray backdrop. And a soundtrack liberated from Philip Glass's creative dynamic accompanies the true confession of sin, chirped out through the millions of squeakers across Rodentia. Played in reverse, and three times slower than the actual speed.

"I slept with ferrets of both genders, stuck my thorn into every bedbug I could get my paws on, and intentionally had sex with bunny rabbits with the purpose of contracting rabbit syphilis, to infect the Inner Union Members. I was deranged. I lost smell of the imperative of the collective. I turned solely within, centering my whole life in pupish delusions of individuality. As a wayward pup, a poor, little lamb who lost his way, I squat here, to proclaim my love and submission to the good shepherd that is the Big Cheese, through his caretakers of the rodents' soul, the All Rodents Extraordinary Commission. May the Big Cheese piss on me so that I may proudly and humbly bear his aroma. I only ask, that now that my soul is clean, I be allowed to die before I revert back to my sickness. Please nuke me in the microwave now, as I still bear in my soul the unconditional love for our great leader, Comrade Steely." At least I squeaked it in my own words.

## Chapter Fifteen

# CROSSING THE GREAT DIVIDE

*T*he divine life is found in the union of the blessed parents. The feminine energy expresses herself in Nature as the Divine Grand Mother, with order Rodentia, our mother species and the prime superorganism, as her blessed daughter. Without a strong masculine figure, we are pups confused about the male role in the family. But the masculine, as guided by the wisdom and courage of its most noble elder statesrat, the Big Cheese, takes that role. Steely has become the new meme, the rooster supreme of the pecking order. And as Nature lives her physical life through the planet Earth, with her chakras emanating her aura, so too does the great superorganism of Rodentia. Our mother, Rodentia, has her own physical presence. Rodentia's body is healthy, but to maintain her health, she must breathe in good, clean, nourishing air, and expel her waste products. Every rat, mouse, beaver, and lemming are a cell functioning as an organ's base element. Cells break down through weakness, whether through cowardice, stupidity, betrayal, or laziness, or from any of the soul sicknesses that lead erring members to turn against

*Nature by turning against Steely. Thus, the body of Rodentia creates through its evolution a waste disposal system, breathing out and excreting bodily wastes. We are that waste. The traitors, spies for Argentina, cowards, and slackers, as well as the stupid, the physically weak, those with a crushed, wounded spirit, all of us are to be excreted by the wisdom of the body's organs.*

A frozen landscape stretches out in the distance on a slightly overcast day in the wintery Yukon. But we rodents in the boxcars can't see that. Crammed together, with no food nor clothes for the frigid nights, a third of the rodents around us are already dead. A frozen chipmunk rests on my right shoulder. A frozen squirrel, arms stretched out, bushy tail twisted into an unnatural shape, rests upon the shoulders of emaciated rats nearby. The "prime rats," as the Dzumbani think of themselves, starve and die with all the other species through this great act of "mercy" given by RexCom. Proof to me that Pike is the real spy and a cat lover. And perhaps, the ultimate rat fink? No . . . that's blasphemy! The Rodents' Commission for Corrective Labor Colonies, or whatever it's called now, has been set up for the salvation for the erring soul. And when the sinners have been made clean in this purgatory, they can take their rightful place in the community of animals as new creatures, cleansed by the ordeal of labor. One's hope will always be on this blessed redemption offered by Nature, the state, our species. Guided by the benevolent power of the Big Cheese, the sewage disposal system is the ways and means of purification. Fear and suffering are its instruments. Focus on the right ideal of the New Natural Rodent is its pathway to freedom, to personal apotheosis. One just has to focus on what a right rat really is, and what a failure of that ideal the rat really has become, by the sin of an independent soul.

In the distance, barbed wire fence appears. Wooden guard towers rise at intervals and the corners. We rodents of every species squeeze together. We push our muzzles through the barbed wire on the windows, hoping to enjoy a new stimulus for our souls.

The boxcar shakes as it stops. After a half hour, the door opens. A RexCom guard pops his head in, silhouetted by the outside light. He greets us with a shriek, "Get out, you bugs!"

With their bayonets, RexCom guards, wearing white stripes across their black headgear, prod us as we scurry out the open door. The brightness of the snow-covered ground blinds us, contrasting the interior of the boxcar. We sniff the air to find our bearings and listen intently to our surroundings as we proceed. Our group moves to an expedient parade ground.

Alongside us, using a megaphone made from a Dinosaur's waxed paper cut, Brother Group Leader Pork-Rot squeals directions at us in some garbled Dzumbani dialect. "Move it! Don't sniff to the right! Don't sniff to the left! Go to the parade ground!"

We continue to our destination. "You filthy humans! You think like humans! You stink like humans! Is that all you are?" shrieks another voice behind us. Most of the guards have either pistols or submachine guns aimed at us. A big, stinky one points his pistol at us.

"March forward! In unison, like good citizens!" he commands.

A field mouse strays out of the pack. Big Stinky pops him dead.

"Don't turn to the right! Don't turn to the left! Come forward!" he continues.

A gopher turns around. Another guard shoots him dead with a submachine gun, as the rodents around him crouch down.

"Keep moving, Nature dammit! Don't turn to the right or left! Face forward! Scamper forward!"

We, the new arrivals, gather on the parade ground before a tree stump. Behind it, a banner of black fabric, with the Rodentian writing system on it, festoons the stump. In Dinosaurian English, it translates as: "The Order and the Union Forgive All Those Who Confess and Forsake Their Ways!"

Upon the stump, a flagpole with the Union flag stands next to a bust of the Big Cheese in his high collared, four-pocketed dzash. Squatting at its right side, our left, and a little in front, is Commandant Executive Commander Pond Scum. Behind him squats his aide-de-camp, Senior Officer Wormwiggle, carrying a thin book in one paw, a black megaphone in the other, and a submachine gun hanging over his shoulder. Wormwiggle stands up on his hind legs, opens the book, and puts the megaphone to his mouth.

"Attention! Attention! Your attention please!"

The prisoners come to order. Wormwiggle continues.

"By order of the first plenum of the fifth congress of the All Rodents Evolutionary Union: Authority over the conduct and discipline of repressed citizens of the Union will rest in the paws of commandants appointed by the All Rodents Extraordinary Commission Central Planning Board." Wormwiggle flips a page. "By order of the executive chief commissar of the All Rodents Extraordinary Commission Central Planning Board, Comrade Executive Commandant Fluffy Cattail hereby authorizes Brother Senior Commander Light-Bearer Pond Scum to be commandant of Corrective Labor Colony #59 of the Greater Liberated Yukon River Drainage. You are all now soldiers of the Corrective Army of Labor. You will answer to us as you are ordered! We hold all authority over your lives! You will follow the species-sanctioned slogans for all repressed citizens. The good Commandant Pond Scum knows that none of you is here by mistake."

Pond Scum steps forward and takes the megaphone out of Wormwiggle's paw.

"Listen to me, you humanistic stink bugs," he commands. "The Union is infallible, as is . . ."—he looks reverently to the bust of Big Cheese—". . . our beloved leader, father of the species, the boss, beloved Comrade GenSec Steely, the Big Cheese."

We, the repressed, lift our heads up to the bust.

"Big Cheese! Big Cheese! Big Cheese!" goes the mantra unto the GenSec's idol of an effigy, as all rodents reverently bow to the idol.

Pond Scum quiets us down. "The Union has found you all to be enemies of the species! And by the good wisdom of the Union and all its organs, you have been placed into my paws for rehabilitation! I hold the power of life and death over all you repressed social parasites! Rodentian dialectical materialism says there is no God! There might not be a supreme being like what some of you delusional mental cases claim to believe in, but here, in the Greater Yukon Valley Drainage, I am your God! I answer only to the Central Committee Planning Board and to our beloved Big Cheese, who's too busy to deal with your issues! Get used to it! Follow my orders! Mine the gold we use to finance our war with your bare paws if you need to! If you're ordered to! And follow the holy maxim of the chief directorate of corrective labor camps and colonies . . . 'Work builds freedom! Work creates repentance!' And the Union stands true on all affairs! Any questions?"

Out of this pack of the repressed, a shivering pack rat stands up, holding himself in a failed attempt to stay warm.

"Good comrade executive commander?" he whistles.

"What do you want?"

The pack rat in the crowd stands higher, on his hind legs. "Good comrade commandant? The AREU is merciful, as well as just, is it not?"

"Brother Belch! Please answer our cold friend's query!"

Behind the pack, a sniper with a big weapon to his shoulder aims at the cold rat. A thunderous report from the weapon shocks every eardrum. The target leaps in the air from the impact of the bullet, and falls back to the snow, feet and paws pointing to the sky, eating death as if it were ambrosia. Pond Scum closes the introduction.

"Any more questions?"

## Chapter Sixteen

# HIERARCHY

The barracks hold the ever-growing number of us inmates, "khyazh" in the camp jargon.

Khyazh works as both masculine and feminine; singular, several, and plural; noun and adjective. The barracks are formed from two dozen hovels made from cardboard, scrap lumber, and slash from the nearby forests. They look like doghouses or toolsheds arranged into three semicircles. In front of the semicircles, two lines of woodshed-like buildings stand, facing each other. From a nearby stream, a pipe uses gravity to bring water into a feeding trough-cum-cistern. Omnipresent wood smoke from each roof of the barracks flows up from the hearths inside to blend its aroma with that of the fir bows nearby. Each hovel works as a censer, offering up a sweet savor of fresh mountain air before the Big Cheese.

We scurry into a shed long ago abandoned by some Dinosaur, to receive our new clothes and new identity. The colony quartermaster crew issues the following to us: one hat with floppy ears and kitten fur lining, one padded jacket made from goat's wool, felt boots made from the lint pulled from human clothes driers, three recycled army trousers with white stripes on the thighs, two tunics in the same style as the trousers, and a bottle cap that will be our food bowl.

The padded wool jackets, thick hats with the big ear flaps, and the summer overalls all have a white strip of cloth on them. We will paint our new names on those strips, and that is who we will be. Our colony names are merely our serial numbers, consisting of a Ratsqueak letter, followed by three numbers. My camp name is *Shay Taleka Kutitzeh Taleka*. Sh-letter 383. We paint our new names on those tags with liberated and improved felt-tip pens, then bundle up. Oxygen, fresh water, and exercise come free of charge here. That other essential—social contact—might go in any direction. For we higher animal life forms, we need that healthy contact with our fellows. That feeling of belonging. How this is going to happen is anybody's guess.

After we receive our things, we scurry through a barracks door made of iron, pulled open and slammed shut with a pulley system, using a Dinosaur brick as a counterbalance. Above it, on a white plywood disk, the number seventeen shines forth in negative; easy to read; a cold welcome to this new home. Two dozen soul-patients fresh to the colony. We all sniff the air, the dirt floor, the walls, and the fear. Around us, bundled up inside the nests made from dried grass and weeds, other khyazh who call this hovel a home mill around, gnawing on the well-chewed woodwork. A Dzumban crawls out of his nest, sniffing in my direction. One thing that hasn't been broken in me . . . my intuition. If anything, it's stronger. And I don't like what I feel.

"Jeemsh! Jeemsh! Get up to Jeemsh heaven where you belong!"

The Dzumban bristles up. I sniff around for a wall, find it by the smell of Shrie fur, and scramble away from the Dzumban, up the wall finding a higher place to stay.

I find another floor, containing several Shries crowding around, gnawing on wood already chewed up. Through our barracks, a fir tree grows from Dzumbani hell, all the way to the chipmunk roost. I find out later the chipmunks use another entrance to avoid the Dzumies.

"Hey, you don't need to take that, brother!" squeaks a Shrie on a stump of a branch. On his tattooed tail is a noticeable circular tat in the shape of a cat's head with several whiskers, done in black ink.

"Bug thorner! Yeah, you, tail hole . . . !" comes the voice of the bristled up Dzumie I avoided.

"Shut your Jeemsh muzzle!" my Shriedaygahba benefactor replies. The Shrie lifts his tail and drops his feces down at the Dzumban.

"Think you're so tough? Come down here and shit in front of me!" responds the bigot below. And I experience déjà vu as though I were in high school. The mentality's the same, if not worse.

The Shrie finishes the spat with, "Scamper off to barracks fourteen, hobo spider!" We sniff one another out, like we rats do, to get to know each other, and size one another up. We two stand on our hind legs, wiggling our whiskers at each other. Then I show my courage as he lets his guard down.

I give the appropriate introduction. "Shay 383. Soul criminal and slacker."

"That's your slave number. What's your real name?"

I have to think about this one. "I think I went by Fearless. I was with the Rocky Mountain Front down in Denver before I found out how Dinosaurian I had become," I offer.

"Yeah, yeah, yeah . . . but what are you in for?"

"I am a traitor and a slacker. And I give pups and married girl rats the old thorn! I am pathetic and deranged . . ."

"Enough of the brainwashing. They're doing it to us because we're Shries." My new friend seems to have kept his healthier ego more intact than I have. I want that.

"Well, they are Dzumbani. What do you expect?" I respond, to keep the conversation going.

"Respect! Honor! I expect to share the power pie with them. Or maybe we should create our own power pie," my friend squeaks.

"I'm with you, brother. But here we are," I answer, not getting a warm reception from him.

"Don't go giving me that Zen cat scat!" he squeals. Probably heard it all before. And it isn't working in the colonies.

"Brother, maybe we're right where we're supposed to be," I add, to be positive.

"Maybe you are. But I'm not letting my pups live in a system that puts them in a socially inferior life. I want them to be proud to be Shries."

"Well, brother, I don't want to upset you. I'm still proud of our species. I'm not going to let a weasel's bitch of a Dzumban bring me down," I answer. Maybe I still have it.

We cut the etheric cords between us, and I go snoop around. I scurry to the wall and gnaw on a small rock sticking out of the mud. The other Shrie stands up on his back legs and sniffs the air.

"Blacksnake?" The Shrie hears his name called.

"Sunflower?" Blacksnake the Shrie replies.

"Just wanted to know that it's you." the other rat scurries around, sniffing the ground.

Blacksnake sniffs me out, testing my boundaries. Anything can set me off at the worst time right now. I bristle up, pushing the fur on my back up with a hiss. Blacksnake backs off a little.

"Haven't lost it, have you?"

"Lost what?" I squeak viciously.

"Your will to live."

"My will to take everybody with me when I die," I throw back at him.

Sunflower sniffs me out with his fur bristled up. "Can I eat him, Sri Blacksnake?" he requests, condescending to me, craven to the apparent alpha Shrie. That's why he addresses him as "Sri," the honorific title used by us, the Shriedaygahbayan. Shrie and Sri come from the same root word, "Shriecheh," which means "noble, clean, worthy of all honor."

Blacksnake answers, "I don't know, Brother Sunflower. He may eat you! Besides, he may make a fine Black Cat."

In life, there is no Chee in lishek. I, Fearless Litzkachew, am alone against the Shrie prison gang we know as the Black Cats. I must show myself worthy of membership.

Sunflower and I hiss at each other, bristled up, in fighting stance. But I feel my spirit draining out into his, and I retreat, trying to maintain eye contact. Sunflower nips at me for emphasis. I bite back, and Sunflower hits me hard with his muzzle. We grab each other's fur with our incisors, and curl up together in a hostile ball with two black tails flopping around. My power dwindles, and I can't scratch him enough. He gets on top of me, dry-humping me, to let me know where we squat with each other.

"You know your place here, Jeemsh," he squeals, releasing his grip. I relax, drawing up one more bit of power, and then lunge for his left ear. He takes charge, attempts to let me know I'm a mere Jeemsh and he's a Shrie. I hit that ear with my incisors, ripping it in half. Sunny tries for my jugular, but I bite his cheek.

We both jump away simultaneously when Blacksnake scampers in. "Alright, give it a rest, you two. Save that hostility for the Dzumbani."

We hiss at each other, causing Blacksnake to bristle up himself. Sunflower backs down to him, more submissive than I'll be to anyone or anything. I slink away, sniffing out a nesting spot for the next few hours. It's no wonder the Dzumbani hold something over us, with this kind of division between us.

Three sheds over, barracks fourteen belches out smoke and a burning flesh stink from its chimney made from a Dinosaur muffler pipe and mud. Inside, the muffler attaches itself to a steel pail where its metal glows from a roaring fire, acting as both heater and crematory. Two mice and a squirrel burn inside the gray glow, pushed alive and fighting back until their fiery deaths.

"Now, if we can get all these Shries into the stove!" comments Craven Slimemold, a beefy Dzumban with a violent offender in good standing and a tail covered with tattoos. The one that defines him is also the longest, running from his rump almost to the point of his tail, letters spelling "Love's a fist in the tail hole!" This tattoo gives the name for his crew here inside the colony: the Lovin' Crew. These rats shamelessly squeal out that Dinosaur song "You've Lost That Lovin' Feeling" every time they rape a new khyazh. In a nest nearby, four other Dzumbani, months old and battle-scarred, hold each other's tails as they prick them with old pins from insulin needles filled with ink. One folds the ink filler from a Dinosaur pen with a needle sticking out of it as he creates a series of dots and dashes on another rat's tail.

Craven runs the entrepreneurial operations inside this colony, so he can get whatever he wants. The burning flesh he smells once belonged to three siblings who withheld the colonial business tax he charges. The sisters who come to the colonies with their families see their pups eaten for protein if they don't prostitute themselves out at his command. At his whim.

Back in barracks seventeen, beneath the loft that we Shries occupy, house mouse Peektah Ricotta cowers. Though he was once the senior staff member of the Supreme Secretariat's Intelligence Committee, now he's just a khyazh like everybody else, suffering under hierarchy's ugly underbelly. He arcs his back in traumatized, unwilling submission to three Dzumbani dry-humping him in violent condescension.

"Do you feel loved now, Mickey?" whistles the Dzumban, with that common slur species-ist rodents use against house mice. Peektah hates it, but he is small, weak of qi, brainy, and introverted. And without backup buddies. So his place in the hierarchy is obvious. "I like you micks," the bigot continues. "I only wish you didn't drink so much."

Jeemsh. Micks. Tapeworms (the slur against gophers because they dwell in the bowels of the Earth)! When will we ever learn?


The aurora borealis shines through the night as though it were a sign from the heavens.

Stretching across the sky from the North all the way to the equator, it would seem. A portent, perhaps? The possible omen gives way to the predawn light from the East, where we rodents find the last of our dinner. I scurry past a gang of my fellow Shries. We all sniff the air, knowing our species by our aroma. Another aroma blends in with ours, that of a chipmunk. Out of the gang's grasp, Soprano Cheekcheekchirblchickle, father to June, the great young hero of the All Rodents Evolutionary Union, leaps into the air, scurrying away from my Shrie brethren with his cheek pouch full of seeds. I scamper to meet this collection of siblings, to find out what gives. Soprano scampers in front of them, until he crawls up a dead tree. All the rats follow him to the tip, leaving him exhausted and dizzy. I come up with them all and come between the chipmunk and the gang. One of the gang, known to everyone by his tone of voice and the simple moniker "Toot," takes charge in the name of Shrie dominance.

"Give us the seeds! You stole 'em like you steal everything. It isn't like you paid for 'em!"

"Brother?" I squeak to the striped squirrel. "What did you do?"

"Nothing!" replies Soprano, the seeds in his jowl pouch keeping his voice constricted. "They are trying to rob me again!"

The gang counters this defensive plea. "Who're you going to believe, brother Shrie? Your own species, or some striped squirrel?"

"The thief wears his prison stripes all the time! Convenient!" comes a voice from my brothers.

"All chipmunks are thieves and tramps. They'll steal right from under your muzzle!" comes another.

"Give us some seeds then go sing a song about it, tramp and thief!" a third shrieks.

Two of them spit out, "Give us your seeds, or we'll make your woman our chippy!"

This is beyond human of us! I must do something about it. I crawl down to the gang, huddling together on the crook of a tree branch.

"Brothers!" I squeak out with as much qi as I can muster. "Isn't this the way we get treated by the Dzumbani?" The gang goes silent.

"What's that got to do with anything?" counters an emaciated member of the gang. "We want some seeds!"

"This isn't about species, tail hole. This is about survival!" adds another, who has scars over his body, an empty left eye socket, and part of his left paw missing.

I may be myopic, but I see a luna moth flapping its wings above all of us. In the middle of winter! Then he lands on the bark. And all is silent. I am insane!


The sun rises in the distance, illuminating our tree. Gone is the exhausted gang of Black Cat wannabes. Fresh after a nap, Soprano takes out a millet seed and chews it with gratitude.

"Thank you, ever so much," he chirps at me in that Least Chipmunchian accent of his.

I raise my muzzle to the striped one. "So much for the unity of the species." I sniff the tree for a way down and get a little gnawing in on the wood before the descent.

"May Mother Rabbit remember you in Her carrot patch!" chirps the chipmunk, in his voice suppressed by the remaining seeds in his pouch. I point my ear at the fellow so I can hear him better, though his gratitude needs no translation. He proceeds down the tree, to find his place on the snow-blanket-ed forest floor. If only the machinery of state would allow his people to hibernate in winter, like Nature intends.


Across the Union, liberated monitors fill themselves with the images of its showcase project, the Great Big Cheese Avenue of Evolution. From the body of water the Dinosaurs named the Great Bear Lake, and the nearby Great Slave Lake, the combination canal/highway/railroad will roll between the two. Great emphasis goes to the workers building such an edifice. Each is a repentant soul criminal, now happy to find salvation through good, hard work. Each looks happy, well fed, and hy-drated, and a scene shows a comfortable dwelling place, with fresh bedding on the floors and cheery posters of our lives in the Union. Then an image appears of stew pouring hot from a big pot into a feeding trough with happy khyazh waiting their turn, preferring one another, showing the most impeccable of manners. Nature knows our colony isn't anything like that!

One evening, I go to the mess hall for breakfast. In the other universe, we forage for our dinner. Here, the Union serves us. Mush made from oats and bean paste falls out onto an aluminum pie plate, so that the five hundred of us have to share. Most of the bean mush ends up feeding maybe sixty of the strongest and feistiest. The rest of us gnaw on tree bark, or just go hungry. We, the gaunt and pissed rodents, sniff the ground for any morsel left behind. Fights break out, like they always do. A scrawny fox squirrel shoves me, and I bite back. Another, I don't know which species, attacks him as well, and I scamper away from the beginning of a fury feeding frenzy, hoping for a late-night dinner when we're fed by the sluice gate. The RLA guard in charge at that time always governs the distribution of the food. And with a good heart, he makes sure we all get enough.

As the feeding frenzy ebbs, the chief of the RexCom security staff joins his subordinate guards and other staff for his dark entertainment. He is dressed in his RexCom finest, with a starched, stiff-collared jacket, black kepi, and shiny black leather belt. He puts a megaphone to his muzzle. "Alright, feeding crew, let 'em fight for the mountain kipper!"

A slab of smoked sucker meat most likely harvested from the nearby river falls down onto the crowd, causing a rush for the salty fillet. The strongest get more of their protein. Then that indescribable bean stuff pours out on the rest. The emaciated rest of breed rodents lap up that delicious pasty stew made from weeds, fish entrails, beans, and grain pressure-cooked through the day. The strongest push their way to the gray stuff on the floor, denying those weaker bodies any hope to reclaim their power. Thus is the way of Nature.

At the mess hall on the other side of the partition separating us from the camp establishment, the RexCom and RLA units get the best food of any unit. Groceries from across the Union go specifically to the guard services of the ROCOCO-LACO colonies. I don't want to think about how the young females sent here have to survive. In the mornings, sometimes I feel Catnip's qi reach out to me, as though she still lives. Maybe she does.

We've become humans in a cage. If you put that stinky species in tight quarters, you know, crowd them in like sardines in a can, they devour one another. Any empathy they once had goes out the burrow entrance. We rodents were never like this before all of this humanism.

The steam whistle blows one long and three short toots calling for assembly outside. All of us scurry out into the bitter air to join escort teams waiting in the cold. Each of the guard teams squats ready for us, in crews of regulation eight guards and twenty-four guard ferrets, assembled in octagonal formation that will escort us to the sluice boxes. We assemble in crews of forty khyazh inside each of the octagonal formations. The head guard of our formation, a Dzumban dressed in full regulation wool coat, hat, and submachine, holds his ferrets back as though they were huge kites in the wind. He whistles, and off we go to our gold-digging job.

## Chapter Seventeen

# VISITATION

G one are the nights when we would stand up at parties, and the all-important rallies to squeak our faith in the Union, when we would spew out great proclamations with evolutionary fervor about the inevitable fall of humanity. Then we would truly believe we would all go out into the liberated gardens and the rubble to build the new Earth. We would love up our girly rats and make so many happy pups. Every RLA fighter would get the pretty, fine-smelling girl prairie dog of his dreams. When the dream becomes nightmare, will we wake up?

I pull a plastic spoon from a backpack, then put it into the sluice box by a sandy edge of a stream, using it as a gold mining pan. With its ever-present rushing sound, the stream provides a comforting lullaby, easing my emotional burden. Hundreds of other rodents covered in rags and furs pull mud out of a trough near the stream as well. Upstream, an effigy two meters tall stands, bearing the title on a piece of cardboard, "Enemy of the Species." Made from plywood, decomposing cardboard, and painted black, white, and blue, the enemy looks like an anthropomorphized mouse, dancing on two hind legs, dressed like a human, a totem of evolution guarding the penitent repressed. Underneath the effigy, a white board with another slogan written in black Ratsqueak letters says, "Death to all traitors who clothe their souls in Dinosaurian humanism!" Along the stream, long streamers of black cloth with white slogans painted on them flap in the wind, encouraging victory in this greatest of all battles here in the colonies.

I see the brightest minds of my generation lose their belief in the Union, and in evolution, crushed out of them by the meat-grinder of the labor camps and colonies. I say this to myself, as I study my siblings in this soul-cleansing arena. For the greatest fight a rat could wage is the war within oneself. The Union is learning this. RexCom enforces and ensures this. All Rodentia is now called to go within itself, for each rat to face one's own doubt and hatred for the order, and to purge one's own being of all doubt in The Big Cheese. Love for him casts out any morbid lack of faith.

In my mind, cameo pictures of various rodents appear over this scene of forced labor in the snow. I see these clearly in my soul. The poetess Clover Cricket, who like so many of the females was forced into prostitution for RexCom officials. The journalist Trout Jump-Happy. The creator of the species' Organic Realism art movement, Moxie Love-Bunny. A 2010 champion of culture sent to the Yukon to dig for gold and die. Maybe I'm just tormenting myself with memories of rodents buried in a mass grave in a crude cemetery. How many will perish in the camps? Only Nature herself knows, as she swallows the dead into her bosom. Maybe a hundred million. More

than the number of our fighters killed in the war this winter.
So many precious shining stones, pulverized in the rock crush-
er, to be poured into concrete for the edifices of the species.
The Correctional Army of Labor has become larger that the
Rodents Liberation Army.


I work on a crew of three Shries, a Dzumban, a very cold gopher, and six prairie dogs. We pull up sludge from the bottom
of the sluice box, then dump it in carts that will go to the ore
pile by the new rail line. Three gangs of my Shrie brethren lay
down rails in the mud and snow not far from us. At least I call
them brothers.

One of the Shries in our crew bumps into me. "Oh, excuse me. You stink like Shay 383," he squeaks as he bristles up.

"Got a problem with that?" I shriek. I got PTSD from this
place and I know how to use it.

"Oh, I'm so sorry, Shay 383. Maybe if I were a Nature-damned chipmunk, you'd show some respect to me!"

"Just do your Nature-damned work!" I try to break off the
bitter soul connection we're sharing when I smell the stink of
the Dzumban next to me. I shriek, "What're you wiggling your
whiskers at?"

"Two little Jeemshees with bad Jeemsh wannabe attitudes!"
he replies.

"You're on your own, feces face!" interjects the Shrie.

"Brothers," I squeak as I stand, incensed by this insanity.
"This, comrades, is the nature of the human. We should rise
above this!" Pup! Where did that come from?

The Dzumban bites me. I squeal as I attack him. So much
for glorious evolutionary awareness. We rip into each other,
neither giving nor taking an inch. Then that Shrie bites each of

us, to keep us agitated. I break away from the Dzumban who then rubs his body in the snow. A thought goes through my soul, one of complete loss of hope . . . this is how we will lose this war. By turning against one another.

Then . . . I still don't quite grasp this but, a luna moth flies over us, circles, then lands on the sluice box! And the moth communicates something to me telepathically. I don't know what it is. It's in the dead of the Yukon winter and the moth doesn't appear to be the least bit cold. But then again, I sport 20/300 eyesight, like most of us rats.

I've been colonized for over a month, at least that's what the grooves on the bark in my barracks tell me. I say "Yes, sir; no, sir!" like a good submissive. Never in my life did I want to be that sort. I always strove for leadership. To be a luminary of my time, my people. To squeak the unsqueakable as comfortably as if I were doing it in my sleep. I notice something about us khyazh. After a while, we adjust to this lifestyle. To a point where any hope of the first universe we broke from will be there again if we survive our time is questionable. My sentence stands at fifteen months, with two already served, and no bad time on my toilet paper, as we call our in-colony records. So, if I don't die between now and spring of next year, I just might be able to face the challenge of being free again.

I was free at one time, not physically free, but free in my soul. I feel the trauma of losing my delicious Catnip, that positive female dynamic in my life. Ripped from me deliberately, crushing the one thing I need most in this scat hole. Hope. Without that, we institutionalize ourselves to survive the humiliation here. This universe becomes our world, our life. Our destiny. And we fulfill the dark underside of Nature's essence by preying on one another. And the ways of the colonies become our ways.

Oh, to sniff that clean tail hole of my earthy girl rat once again! I still fantasize about tasting her again. So maybe hope does struggle for life within my own soul. I sense in what little intuition I have that she's still alive, still loving me. We betrayed each other. That's when the Steely clique achieves its strongest victory. Catnip, if you can sense the vibes of my spirit, I still love you. Let's be together, no matter what we did. Let's take that crappy clique's victory and turn it into their fatal mistake!

RLA fighters nearby scamper over, grabbing each one of us.

"He started it!" shrieks the troublemaking Dzumban.

"Liar! Traitor! Kitten!" I bite back.

The fighters wrap twist ties around my front and back paws, as the Shrie gazes at me in contempt while he gnaws the sluice box.

My sentence is to go to the dreaded white box for a week. RexCom guards take over from the fighters and shove me into a metal box once painted white, containing an annoying white light burning in a corner niche. Off go the twist ties, and I sniff out a place to squat without being bothered. The light heats up the box, and a constant drip of water provides hydration. Maybe I needed a break.

## Chapter Eighteen

# WHITE BOX

The white box is a treat. At least, the first night of it. I have to remain standing, silent, and can only drink and piss on the hour. Other than that, I squat here, in this box, alone with myself.

I feel something, an idea. I have an emotion for an idea I learned then forgot . . . I don't know, months ago. With all this solitude, I choose to *not think*. Only for say, five minutes. That's enough. I stop my thought processes. Except, I allow myself to envision a clock ticking away the seconds. I take a break after I count out five minutes. My mind rushes forward with the junkiest thoughts I ever could conjure, and with them feelings of anger, hopelessness, and only Nature knows.

So I mark fifteen minutes. I quiet myself down and begin.

I notice my soul senses my surroundings despite the lack of variety. My senses feel my body's organs. Oh, Excreta! *I'm in a creek!* I know exactly where I am!

My soul returns to my family home in the Colorado mountains, to the fresh air and silence undisturbed by the encroachment of our enemy. Beyond the dead tree that sheltered our lives are the nearby gardens where a rat's favorite vegetable, brussels sprouts, grow proudly yet threatened by the bondage of Dinosaurian genetic modification. Here my siblings and I collected the tiny cabbage-like heads. The flavor of the cooked vegetable, mingling with its aroma, and that of my extended family, imprinted on my soul and will never be forgotten nor rejected. All of us siblings would join other rats in the two foraging times of the night: late evening, and before sunup.

Buttercup, my little sister from another mother, loved to play together with me in the morning twilight by the stream out back. With a younger sibling's undying trust, Buttercup trusted me with her life. I think I was a young adult at the time, educated, active, and scrappy. I was the last born of our mother's first litter, but I could and would still hold myself with an alpha's leadership bearing. And I made sure I was always true to my name. I was never a bully, but I never let the sniping and snarky jabs of the pecking order leave any of my fellow Shries wounded or unavenged. In our lishek, that extended family of thirty to seventy rodents, I became an honored example of service. We also use lishek as the name of a similar size RLA unit. I squat in gratitude for my upbringing in and service to our lishek, defender of the weak and marginalized, the go-to rat for decency, wisdom, and empathy. Not to toot my own horn, as the Dinosaurs say, but that was how I was.

One early morning, that darkest of all the dawns in my many months of life, Buttercup and I gathered seeds and roots near the stream we so loved. Ending the night's foraging before the sun would break over the distant, invisible prairie, we sniffed at the earth, and enjoyed each other's presence. Together, we bathed in gratitude to know our place within these mountains our lishek called home.

A garter snake slithered up behind us, fresh from its winter burrow under an old dead stump, covered with a thin veneer of bright green moss. That legless relative of humanity came right up behind Buttercup. Its tongue flicked at her as she sensed its malevolent presence. This is all coming back to me like it's happening now. I see this all in my soul. Like a nightmare. I hear her squeak a distress chirp right to me. I stood up to sniff the air for her location. She scampered into the stream when the serpent lunged for her, then the tip of its tail slapped me in the muzzle. I jumped at his blurry image and got ahold of the reptile's tail. I bit into that scaly hide and dug into it with my claws. I kept biting into the snake's flesh, gnawing into it to find its spine. But I lost all contact with Buttercup. Others smelled her in the water and later told me she floundered in the stream, fighting the current with her natural ability to tread water. The snake attacked me with its forked-tongued mouth. That's when I bit the snake again, getting it right on the nose. The two of us squirmed, splashed around, and then the snake slithered away. I trod the water as I floated downstream, alone now, without attacker or sister. I kept chirping out a locating call to her. Then I whistled another call. Only the babble of the rushing stream answered. Then I heard other rats squeaking from the bank. When I got to the dry ground, I called again with a high-pitched chirp, then scampered downstream along the bank. With shrill, shrieky whistles, Buttercup's name went across the bubbling babble of the mountain water, without response.

As the nights went by, our sister was remembered by the four litters who lived within our lishek. Buttercup's mother keened with a hideous, unnerving chirp of sorrow for her pup, my beloved sibling, who I couldn't save. Never would she find lasting solace.

I keep taking my time with all of this silent soul work. I'm enjoying being in trouble with the guards! This is the best I've felt since my reality splintered into a million pieces. Then I heard, "You are under arrest!" This soul peace is a joy! The process is a sorrow! I find both demand my attention.

Then, feces! The door swings open and an officer scampers in. And I know why he's here before he opens his muzzle.

"Shay 383! Your week is up! Scamper out of the box and get your uniform back on," the officer will say. And does!

My escorts, eight RLA fighters assigned to the best-fed duty in the service and four of their guard ferrets, take me back to barracks seventeen.

"Get back to Jeemsh heaven, you stinking Jeemsh piece of scat!" Thus is the familiar greeting of the species-ist Dzumban.

When I get to my old nesting spot, Toot is lying right in what was my only natural escape from this place. His greeting flows like an earthy, yet edgy, urban tone poem, "Get the thorn away from me, you bug-thorning chipmunk lover." Funny, I'm so okay with his hostility. And I bear a beautiful empathy for him. And for the troubled Dzumie downstairs.

Empathy. It feels so natural. I like it! I feel this empathy flow out to our Dzumban neighbor in the basement who was the first to greet me. All Dzumbani! All of us, as well. Then I remember my sister Buttercup and I smell Catnip's delicious aroma. And our Dzumban comrade Cappuccino flows through my soul. And I feel grounded to our Earth. Her resonance flows through me like my mother's love. I bear an intuitive knowledge flowing throughout my whole being that there is power, both within and from beyond oneself, that I, Fearless Litzkachew, can access. And never again will I let that which I love to perish without a fight.

## Chapter Nineteen

# RABBITARIA

Our work crew scurries past the sluice box. The early morning twilight shares the sky with the dancing aurora borealis. I may be blind in one eye, and I can't see out the other, but I sense those heavenly lights above. We pass a pile of our dead, about two dozen of our fallen siblings from the smell of it. Even though they're frozen, we rodents can pick up their putrescence.

I defy death by machine gun fire with a simple deviation from the path, yet the guards and their watch ferrets don't really notice. One ferret steps up to me, sniffs me out, and returns to the march as though he couldn't care less.

And now I stray from our crew to squat by the stream feeding the sluice box. I sense spirits in the water of this stream. Perhaps the water absorbed the qi from souls who've died building this gold mine for the pinnacle, founded upon the broken bodies and souls of the masses. And then I get the impression that living beings hop by my side.

"Fearless Litzkachew!" comes a coherent voice from the babbling stream. I sniff the air in the direction of the water. Then I see with a clarity not possible for the rodent eyes. Before me, an untold host of rabbits . . .

"Hares!" comes a voice from the host of off-white jackrabbits with black prong-horned antlers between their long black-tipped ears. Heavenly jackalopes. I stand corrected on the rabbit thing.

"I am a rabbit!" I behold the glory of a big brown rabbit, the alpha and the omega in the midst of the jackalopes. In my heart, I fall on all fours (I'm already on them, anyway), burying my head in the water-sprayed gravel. Fear from some unknown source flows through me yet I feel no threat attached to it.

"Who are you, lord?" I offer to the unknown with a meek squeak.

"Who am I? Please give me the name my beloved Soprano refers to me." The voice doesn't bear any malice in it, but the presence so strongly vibrates that I can't help feeling a little menaced.

"Lord, would you be the Big Bunny?"

"You say that I am," comes the answer from the presence.

I feel so overwhelmed I want to scurry away. Then the presence relaxes, lessening its intensity.

"I'm speechless, lord," I confess.

"Words project power. Don't be afraid, Fearless. You are known by my father, and my mother. And my sister will be with you. If you value her." Now I feel the Big Bunny's spirit to be inviting, affable. I haven't felt affability for a long time. Affability and sympathy can be found only in the dictionary, somewhere between "ad nauseum" and "suicide." And there ain't no dictionaries in the ROCOCOLACO colonies.

I'm completely beyond words. But then, a beautiful rose-colored light bathes us all. I can't even see shades of red! But I can now. I see white, glorious light in the middle of the jackalopes, above Big Bunny. I see in all my being a beautiful white rabbit, clothed in a rose-colored velvet robe, with her ears standing up, bearing a crown of pink roses around those blessed white ears.

The phantasm fades from view, then I smell my surroundings. I haven't missed a step with my crew.


Up in the nesting place the Cheekcheekchirblchickle family calls home, I relate what happened. Maybe he knows what it's all about.

"Brother, ever since I went to the box, things like this . . . I don't know. I'd say, they *seem* to be happening," I share, trying to relate the unrelatable.

"I've never had the Big Bunny talk to me," chirps the chipmunk, almost with envy, I sense.

"Well, Hell's bells, Brother Chipmunk. I never asked for it!" I spew in frustration.

"I have, and I never received."

"That ain't my fault!" I cheep in exasperation. I hope this doesn't turn into a religious argument. I already feel the peace I had lift from this conversation.

The chipmunk makes some squabbly sounds and tries to ignore me. Then he flicks his tail and chirps bitterly, "Get out!"

I slither down to the Black Cat den, as I call our section of the barracks. None of my fellow Shries wants to acknowledge me. Yet the tension I felt after meeting with Soprano eases.

Life and death go on in the colony. New arrivals show up, replacing the dead. I stay alive, and now I work on something new. Each day I make it a point to take between five and fifteen minutes and to breathe deep, breathing in the golden light of love and healing into the core of my body, then I breathe it up my tail and over my spine to the top of my head. The light becomes a circle of life for me as I feel a connection to Mother Earth, and this moment. I focus on the moment, listen to the beauty of the water flowing through the sluice box, and appreciate the fresh air that fills my lungs. And something else resonates in me. I don't know why but I feel gratitude for these things, these simple pleasures. The ability to breathe, to drink fresh healthy water, to find moments we can ground ourselves into Earth and Nature; these become my treasures. Fresh water, living water, flowing before us with a meditative ambience. We must request permission to drink at the sluice box, but we can drink a river up if we're that thirsty. I like to focus on the moment, and when I do so at the sluice box, I focus on the sound of the rushing water. I quiet myself knowing I live rooted to the union of the Earth and the divine.

But one wound may never heal. My memories of the girl rat I love. Catnip has never left my soul. I have no way of knowing if she's alive, but at times here in the colony, I sense her presence. Perhaps she's the thorn garage for some Dzumban criminal kingpin who's into Shries. A lot of those hypocrites are! I still think about Cappuccino. She's either a hero of the AREU, or a martyr. She would give her all to our Rodentia. I wonder whatever happened to her. Nature forbid she crossed over to this side of the universal divide.

Defilement. Pollution. That's what goes on here in the colonies. ROCOCOLACO is the most unnatural abomination wrought by the paw of Rodentia. I have a tattoo on my tail I hope will be a part of the healing of our collective species. It shows bare incisors with the caption "Our Rodentia. Love her like that special someone, treat her like a dear mother." I paid twenty oats to a field mouse to do the work. It's small. Maybe that's the love worth investing in? So, this is our reality. We love our Earth. So much so that we turn on one another to keep the big other from destroying our hopes in Rodentia. Maybe we're all enemies of the species.

## Chapter Twenty

# COLONY JUSTICE

Meanwhile back in the prime universe, Steely pisses on the Black Guards banner, then presents it to the unit leadership staff of the 3rd Division of the 13th Route Army, the first division awarded the title of Black Guards. A seven-month-old squirrel, too young to be cowardly, too wise to show fear, with a liberated bandage strip over the wound in his face, accepts the sacred banner exuding the aroma of the Big Cheese. Bullets from human firearms buzz overhead.

In the magnificent brain of the Big Cheese, almost large enough to overfill a teaspoon, a wise leader never exposes himself to the dangers of combat. Yet Steely squats with the brave fighters against humanity. Behind a liberated convenience store, with the rumble and high-pitched crack of gun fire accompanying the impromptu ceremony, Steely presents himself as the rightful alpha male of the whole taxonomic order, hoping no one senses his terror. Snow dusts the cityscape, falling gently upon the ice. A gentle wind blows over the frozen corpses of what had been custodians, entrepreneurs, alpha humans, bottom-feeders. Boy and girl humans. Young, old, and in between. The breeze carries away the acrid smoke from burned cars and buildings, bringing with it cool air filled with oxygen, refreshing and enlivening.

"Comrades! Siblings! Fellow evolutionaries! I want to express my deepest gratitude to you for your efforts. All of we animals are in a fight for survival against humanity. Our planet will thank you in her resonance for all you are doing. And you fighters of the 3rd Division can proudly call yourselves Guards! You are the guardians of evolution. I end this with . . ."—an explosion puts an exclamation mark on Steely's speech—". . . I have to scamper! I thank you again."

Steely scurries away from the ceremony with his entourage and his faithful RLA watchdog, Comrade Feisty Firebee, chief of staff for the RLA Supreme Command nearby. That fellow Dzumban, with his thinly shrouded contempt for the other species of the order, scurries up to the Big Cheese preventing any attack from a traitor or a spy. A mortar round explodes a block away.

"We're never doing this again, Firebee," chirps the GenSec.

"Doing what, Beloved Comrade Steely?" asks Comrade Feisty. More bullets buzz overhead, blowing pieces of concrete off buildings that roll around near the entourage. A chunk of concrete bounces between them and an armored eight-wheeled executive fighting vehicle that will take them away from all this horror they created.

"Being anywhere near this insanity."

One morning, as dawn interrupts the beautiful night with its pale light from the East, I slowly scurry away from the escort to the entry to our barracks, when some Dzumbani scamper to me from the middle of nowhere.

"Enemy of the species! Yes you, bug thorner!" one shrieks at me, as the gang grabs me.

"You obviously have the wrong rat!" I respond.

"Shay 383! You're the right one!" another spits at me. "Come on, you cockroach!" The tail holes fasten their incisors on my padded jacket then tug me toward somewhere only they know. I bite one of the paws I feel on me, but I'm outnumbered.

Those bug thorners pull me into barracks fourteen. A pups' choir sings a song on the PA system reverberating across the snow outside and through the smoke-smelling barracks interior. Inside, a Dzumban stands up among the others. I can smell his arrogance better than I can see his muzzle.

"What the thorn did you bring in?" he squeals.

One of the Dzumbani lifts his tail as he approaches that arrogance in fur. "Most Honorable Craven. May we present to you enemy of the species Shay 383?"

"Bring the cockroach!" Craven licks his thorn, then points his muzzle to another Dzumban on the bunk overlooking the stove. Sticking out through the roof, a muffler pipe works as the stove's smokestack. The stove has its top open so that heat rises right out. The Dzumban comes down from the bunk to join the fury gang, and I smell her pheromones.

"Cappuccino!" I shriek.

The gang around me bites me mercilessly. "Shut your muzzle!" they squeak viciously.

"Shut your muzzles!" commands the arrogance-wreaking Craven. Slowly and deliberately he scurries up to me, in command of his surroundings, emphasizing his alpha position. "I haven't smelled you before," he purrs at me, the way I would when Catnip and I would make love. He wants to make violence. "Oh, pretty buttercup. You smell so delicious," he coos, then he licks my ear, and I bite his muzzle. Then I bite him with, "Traitor!"

He reels back, and I sense his months of dominance and having everyone else do his work has softened him. He composes himself, to save muzzle in front of his sycophants. "You are a naughty little enemy of the species. I like you. I think you're setting me on fire on the inside."

My time is now! The sycophants relax just enough! With every bit of my power, I bound out of their hold and scamper up to the bunk over the stove. Cappuccino follows me.

"Absolutely fabulous! We can throw that traitor into the stove!" squeals Craven.

"Don't you want to hold a trial for him, Most Honorable Craven?"

"Why? He's guilty of holding back his in-colony tax! Shay 383! Don't tell me no one told you that you owe the in-colony administration a tenth or more of your wage increase?"

I hiss out, "We don't get paid *excreta* here! And that's what I thorning owe you! Cat scat!"

"Well, that's quite correctable. You can pay me in thorny love! Ask Dah 697 up there."

Cappuccino, with the slave name Dah 697, sniffs me out and softens in her stance. "Comrade. You'll get used to it soon enough," she says.

"We'll lose the war with this attitude!" I squeal at her.

The room erupts in laughter. "No one here gives a cat scat about your war for evolution!" chatters Craven. "We are evolution's end! Evolve!"

Here I squat, muzzle to muzzle with the true New Natural Rodent. Comrade Cappuccino. Dzumban, as opposed to me, the Shrie. She's submissive to authority, as the colony kingpin thorns everybody into submission. Our beloved Earth will soon become Planet ROCOCOLACO, complete with its hierarchy of guards, vanquished kingpins, and submissives. Then *we* will be the Dinosaurs.

"Come get me yourself, you fat piglet!" I viciously chirp at Craven. The imperative of this situation drives me to do or die. And with it all our hopes and sacrifice. "You can't do scat without your sycophants!"

"I don't need to!" replies the alpha Craven. "Get the kitty!"

That camp slur "kitty"—I don't even want to describe what it means—sets me off even more. Craven's craven sycophants scamper up the bunk. I drop off the edge right above the stove below me and crawl around under the bunk. I drop to some bare space under me and attack Craven, who loses his alpha presence. I chase him back up to the bunk.

Out of the corner of my eye, I clearly see the luna moth I saw earlier. She sends a telepathic message to me: "We're with you, Brother Fearless."

"Who's 'we,' Comrade Moth?" I chirp, taking everyone by surprise.

"You'll know in time," comes the reply.

"Sibling Luna Moth, how shall I address you?" I inquire.

"I am *the* luna moth." Sounds simple enough.

All the other rodents seem stunned. At the edge of the bunk, I bite Craven. He leaps away from me as he squeals in terror. I watch him drop out of view as I get to the edge of the bunk, then crawl under it hearing the fire in the stove accelerate. Hanging under the bunk, I can actually see the fire burning Craven's body, with only his tail sticking out of the fire. The smell of his burning fur in the stove drifts up to me, like a delicious roasted piglet at a holiday feast.

"Save him! Quick!" I scream in terror. The sycophants scamper to the edge to smell their leader cooking in the stove.

"It's Craven! Save him!" I shriek, and the sycophants oblige. As one unit they dive down onto the hot stove, grab Craven's tail, and pull him out of the flames as their paws sizzle on the red-hot metal and stone. Each and every one of them is burned. Except for the hypnotized one, Cappuccino. I drop to the floor, and grab her by the scruff of the neck, as if she were my naughty pup. I pull her out of barracks fourteen, and practically carry her to ours. Behind me, the sycophants drag their burned god into the snow, preferring his healing to theirs, as the sun rises in the East.

Inside barracks seventeen, I push Cappuccino past that species-ist in the basement. He explodes in insanity as I've never experienced from him before. "What are you doing with that Dzumie girl?"

"He's going to thorn 'er ass as a warm-up for you!" says one of my Shrie neighbors.

I push the Dzumie girl up into our section, past the poster of rodents together in unity, squatting under the caption "All Rodents Together are One Species!" I used to believe that, too.

Speciesism. Rodentia's dirty little secret. No mere Bogey Mouse.

"What in Nature's white winter are you doing with a Dzumie in *Jeemshy heaven?*" squeals Toot, the reverse species-ist. This stops me in my tracks.

"We aren't Jeemsh!" I shriek. "We're *Shries!*" Cappuccino gnaws on the entryway like it's her last chew. After a calm settles on the whole barracks, I continue with my lecture. "We're all siblings! Rodents! Comrades!"

"But you're an enemy of the species! That's why you're here!" Toot squeaks at me, like an arrogant mouse. "We're outlaws!"

I motion to my spot in the nest where I sleep. "Cappuccino. Take my spot for your nest."

"My name is Dah 697!" comes her monotone reply. This is going to be hard.

## Chapter Twenty-One

# AWAKENING

Craven peeps out a miserable lament, resonating with fallen egotism. His crew rolls him over and over in the snow, pushing him with their heads. They gingerly paw the snow with cremated paws, losing digits with each bad move of their blistered forelimbs. Together, the tormented chirps and peeps dance across the snow in the early morning twilight, contributing to the misery of this unholy place.

Craven's whole crew, except for Cappuccino, their sexual meat, suffers together out in a dark circle upon the light gray snow. Craven can't think of anything but his pain and shock, now clouded over with trauma's delirium. This one-time crew power maker and breaker impotently shivers in winter's cold breath, helpless, defenseless.

I scrounge up some dry grasses and a few pine needles for my bedding. Dah 697 rests comfortably in my nest, as though it were hers. Blacksnake sniffs around my space. He bristles up a little at her foreign odor.

"What's a Dzumie Jeemsh doing in our nest?" he asks.

"Sleeping," I respond.

"You're not thorning that, now, are you?"

"Why is it when male and female get together, it always has to be about thorning sex?" I chirp, exasperated by the ignorance I smell in our species. "I met her on the battlefield, and she's an asset to us."

Blacksnake smooths his fur and gnaws the chewed-up branch above us. The pine smell fills our space. "I don't want her here," he states, more as an afterthought, or habit.

"Well, can she just sleep a few hours before we send her on her way?" I ask.

Blacksnake moves back to his nest. I sense . . . a peaceful breeze enveloping me. Not wind, but something else. "Blacksnake," I call to my Shrie brother. "Craven's rolling around in the snow. The colony kingpin can't even lick his own tail hole."

"What's that supposed to mean?" he asks.

"He tried to rape me tonight. And that's why I have the Dzumban sister . . ."

"She ain't your sister!" he interjects.

"Would you be so Shrie as to cut the species-ist cat scat and *let me finish!*" I shriek, PTSD doing the squeaking for me now. Like a gentle snow carpeting a forest floor, silence fills our space. Then it is interrupted by the gnawing sound of the Dzumies in the basement. ". . . As I was squeaking, the Craven crew can't defend itself. They're burned really badly, and they can't fight back."

"So?"

"So if we go over to barracks fourteen *right now*, we can kill and eat them. And sell their pre-cooked meat to some of the others."

Blacksnake sniffs out the Black Cat crew in our barracks. Toot, Pest, maybe nine others whose names I don't know, all slowly sniff the air, wiggling their whiskers in Blacksnake's authoritative cognizance. "Brothers," he addresses them. "We got fresh meat in the snow. Follow me."

We crawl over the gnawing Dzumies in the basement, out onto the yard. Blacksnake sniffs at me, "Shay 683, lead the way!" Wasn't I supposed to be Shay *383*?

I sniff out the way to barracks fourteen, then point my muzzle in that direction. The Black Cats hop over the snow with me, a pod of black dolphins swimming in this sea of crystalized water. Upon the snow's surface, the peeping lamentations of the wounded Craven crew direct us to them.

We stop at their circle of misery. I squat upright. "Craven, you ignorant slut! You called me to lick your thorn, and now I'm here to gnaw it off!"

"I'll run this show," Blacksnake interjects. "Black Cats!"

The Shrie crew squats in attention to Blacksnake, as the burned Dzumies shiver in horror at their fate. Blacksnake sniffs the Dzumies, taking a nip out of the closest one. The wounded chirp out an appeal for help, which drifts across the snow into oblivion.

"Water . . . water," coos the severely wounded Craven, not grasping the seriousness of his situation.

"If there's one thing good about a Dzumie, it's that they taste good when they're cooked!" exclaims Pest.

"Let's eat!" shrieks Blacksnake.

We all dive in on these burned offerings to the dark spirits of ROCOCOLACO, feasting on their flesh as we save some thighs and other parts for the in-house black market.

The sun appears through the breaking cloud cover, shining a warm light upon us, as if Nature herself gives her approval. We make our way back as some guards sniff out the gnawed bones left behind. Those guards get the best food in the Union, so they don't have a big appetite for rat meat.

We sleep well on full bellies, not a common experience in the colony. The clanging of the sundown bell rings throughout the barracks. Most of us shake our heads in the first minutes of wakefulness, where the soul comes back into its body from the realm of night dreams. We have a while to eat our salted minnow meat and raw rolled oats before the ferrets and their handlers escort us off to the gold digging.

I approach Blacksnake. Something in my countenance strikes him funny.

"You're never going to be a Black Cat, Shay 683," he remarks out of the blue.

"Is it because I use my soul for myself? Without the approval of some mob?" I answer.

"The boys don't want you. You act too educated."

"I'm self-educated. I hated all six nights of school."

"At least you had that much. You sure learned a lot in that time."

I pause, then share with him: "I love learning. But I hate anyone one else squeaking what I have to know. How to feel. My soul is my own."

"All that inquisitive stuff brought you here, I bet."

"No," I answer, "I would say all my inquisitive love for learning sets me free. This place is a failure in our collective approach."

"Before I got here, I wanted to read and write. But my future is set."

"No, it's not," I counter, trying to be a help.

"Oh, birds. After all this 'enemy of the species' stuff, we Shries will always be the . . ."

"No! That's the problem right there!" I sense a shift in his soul with that rebuke.

"We're at the bottom now. But this is where we redefine ourselves. I refuse to be just another khyazh in my own soulscape. And I don't want to be alone in this anymore either. I want to see us as Shries, as *rodents*, come up out of that 'Jeemsh' mentality."

The assembly bell rings out its five-minute warning. I get my clothes for the day together, then with the assembly bell, I go out into the cold, to organize myself with a work crew and feel alone. As usual.

## Chapter Twenty-Two

# BIRTH OF A COMMUNITY

The Black Cats approach a lone Dzumban, one of those from the basement. False dawn fills the tree line by the sluice box with just enough light to see, but not enough to betray any movement. The guards and their ferrets occupy themselves with some dispute between a gang of squirrels and two beavers. The Dzumban slinks away, mouthy in the basement, but trying to be unobtrusive out here in the open.

The anticipation torments us worse than the actual event. The Dzumban crawls onto the sluice box's edge, then scampers toward the section where we're panning gold. The Black Cats pounce onto the edge in front of him, driving him away from the section. One slightly big Dzumban, with a half dozen Shries in tow, goes up to the top edge of the sluice box like a monorail of gray and black. Then that ratty monorail derails, spilling all into the snow beyond visual range and earshot.

I scurry down into the sluice box to spoon out the sludge. I smell blood on the water. Blacksnake scurries up to me with his plastic spoon on his back.

"I don't like it. At all," Blacksnake comments, sniffing the air upstream.

"I think we might be one Dzumban less," I offer.

"That bigot had a big mouth like the rest of his kind. I wonder how he's doing alone." Blacksnake asks that question as though he has the answer already.

I taste blood in the water. A rat's tail flows under my muzzle. I sniff it out, and see the top part of a body above the water, pushed downstream by the current. Blacksnake sniffs out the body with his whiskers bouncing over the corpse.

"Dzumban! Smells like he might even be alive." Blacksnake continues to check out the rat.

I know better than to recommend we try to save this foreign rat, whose species condescends ours. And maybe Blacksnake knows all about this rat dying already. Murder goes on here in the colony quite regularly; few get sent to the cellar where the microwave oven does its work. It's not unusual to come across a sibling who has been garroted then left to rot hanging on the natural gibbet of a tree branch. And not from an execution sanctioned by the colony commandant.

I scrape the bottom of the sluice box, then put the sludge-filled spoon into my mouth. At the sludge heap, I dump it as the sludge relocation crew begins to drag it off. Blacksnake sets his spoonful of sludge down, then rubs his muzzle in true ratty form.

"I want you to teach me, Shay 683."

His request causes us both to pause from our enslaved

circumstances and enter into the here and now. I respond, "What would you like to learn?"

"Teach me to read and write." Some preconceived judgment rises inside my soul. Nah . . . he wouldn't ask what my ears just heard him say. I'm too smart to think that. "You learned how to do it. I could be jealous of you, or I could learn it myself."

I fall silent inside myself. I'd love to set up something in the colony where we could use this nightmare as an opportunity, creating a beneficial experience. "Yeah, maybe. No . . . I don't know." I don't know what I'm squeaking.

"You're confused, rat. Yes or no. Answer me." Blacksnake's response makes sense.

I pause again. But that wasn't helping before. Then I add, "I want to teach you how to read and write."

"Then do it."

"Okay then, we'll do it,"

The weeks go on. Our work nights shorten with the returning sunlight, and with it, warmer air blows across our whiskers. The workloads shift back and forth. For now we're working on the finishing touches for the rail link to the outside world. But a new feeling about this place caresses my soul. If I can take a nightmare like this and make it work for good, imagine what can be done in the real world.

Blacksnake and I squat before a list of letters used in Standard Ratsqueak. He uses a twig to write out a full sentence, stating, "We are all rodents, siblings in the family of Nature." Then, he starts a conversation in the dirt. "Letters of Ratsqueak use the palm, the knuckle, and the claw."

"Good," I write. Then I ask in writing, "And the tail?"

"What's that?" he chirps.

"Think about the sound. In fact, go ahead and scribble it out . . . 'Khesha.'"

"*Khe . . . eh . . . shay . . . schwa . . . khesha*! Tail!" he squeals triumphantly. This grabs the attention of the other Black Cats.

Pest scurries over, curious about Blacksnake's triumph. I write something a little harder. As I do, I tell him, "This will build your skillset a little more." Two other brothers come over to investigate.

On the ground, I start to write out a phrase, then stop myself. "Blacksnake," I dictate. "Write out this phrase . . . 'My writing will empower me.' Think of each sound." Blacksnake writes out the Leh-Shay-Eeh of the first-person possessive pronoun. Then he spells out "writing" correctly. He adds the prefix making the next verb future tense, but he stops to think about our word meaning empower. I write out, "Think how it sounds."

Blacksnake spells out the rest of the phrase in proper Ratsqueak. I'm elated, and the small crowd takes note.

"Why do you do that? You'll never be anything but a Jeemsh," comes a voice from the back. Everyone sniffs out the source of the condescension. Sniffing the air behind them, Cappuccino approaches, with a personal vibration that seems to me to be weaker than I've ever felt from her.

"I'll thorn that prissy-ass Dzumban tail hole you got!" Toot growls the slur with a malignant peep. I sense no compassion for her from any of the other Shries at this moment. But then my student surprises me.

"Brethren!" Blacksnake calls, "We aren't going to be Jeemsh in our own souls. Don't let that slut bother you. We're only Jeemsh if we believe we are. I'm a Shrie! Proud of it! And at this moment, I will not answer Nature's call to kill that sow bug." A pause quiets us all, then he adds, "And neither are any of you! And keep your Nature-damned thorns to yourselves!"

"And may I add, save those thorns for the most delicious girly rats on Earth, our Shrie women!" Pest proclaims, standing up on his hind legs.

The small crowd scurries away, and Cappuccino slinks over to her nest that used to be mine.

The next morning, during the time I work with Blacksnake on his reading skills, I approach both him and Cappuccino together. She's listening to him as he reads from a sheet of paper stolen from a book.

"And after Sheep Poker declared war against Nature . . ." he reads slowly, just like he does with me. He's coming along fine with his pronunciation. Fortunately for all of us, Ratsqueak is phonetic.

Cappuccino peaceably interjects, "What does our Great Leader do?"

"He arrests all the enemies of the species and sends them here," answers Blacksnake.

"That's right. Maybe we're all enemies," she mournfully chirps.

"Sister, your problem is that you lost all self-respect." Blacksnake's response washes over her, and she tries to find a place in the conversation to scamper out.

"Cappuccino," I call. "You've surrendered your power. You need to get your qi back."

"Don't rub it in!" she shrieks. Sounds like healing to me.

"No, you got to listen. I've been looking for you since that night we saved our wounded on that snowy field covered in burning fighters. I've wanted you to play a service role in our Union with me since that night," I confide.

"What do you want out of me? You're not of my species. You sure aren't going to be my father!" she snaps back.

"I want us to heal Nature. I think you can play a big role in that."

She turns to Blacksnake who sniffs at her, "Let's keep reading, alright? And . . . our Glorious Leader Steely . . ."

I back away to leave them alone. But it is a consolation that they are working together.

# Chapter Twenty-Three

# SALON

Blacksnake isn't the only one who wants to read. Most of the Black Cats either have some skill in reading and writing, or they want to learn. Enough so, that they show up at the new after-work mental power hour we've created for ourselves. At this hour, we spend time scribbling sentences and paragraphs in the dirt and read passages out loud.

One night, a Golden-mantled ground squirrel with stripes on its back scurries up to us as we begin to work.

"Siblings," he greets us, "I would like to join your study group. Do you . . ."

"No squirrels!" squeals one of the Black Cats.

"Come on, give the squirrel a chance," Blacksnake interjects.

I step in. "We don't even know you, squirrel. Would you be so kind as to tell us who you are?"

"I am Spunky Kcherkcherktesherk," he says, hesitantly. "I watched you rats . . . I hope you can understand me . . . but I see something positive coming through this collection of minds ." His squirrelly accent does get in the way, but I can read his spirit. I sense no alarm in my intuition as he chirps. Just his trauma.

"Brother Spunky, you're coming to mind, but I just can't place who you are," I mention.

Spunky the ground squirrel humbly offers, "I was a senior fellow in a hoveling co-operative. Years ago, when I was just a pup, I stepped into the point of view of some Dinosaur's camera. I became a meme. But it was the most beautiful portrait of a rodent I've ever seen." The luna moth flicks her wings around this fellow. I see here in my mind's eye, yet I can't see it physically.

Spunky scampers away, and I feel relieved. But I remember something about him. I whistle at him, "Spunky! Ground squirrel with the Golden-mantled accent! Was that picture the only reason you're here?"

He stops, standing up to flick his busy tail at me. "You're AREU, are you not?"

"I don't know now. I was," I reply.

"I am your enemy!"

"Not if I say you're not!"

Spunky scurries over to me. "Squeak it! You hate the Co-Op Leagues!"

That was it. This is Spunky Kcherkcherktesherk! "Spunky! Do you know which Spunky you are?" I bleat like a schoolgirl meeting the Thin White Duke.

"I should hope so! I never will give my power away to your collectivist system!" he whistles.

"I thought you were an Inner Union member. I saw it on television."

"*Was*. The longer I worked for the AREU, the more I knew it was failing at everything it squatted for."

"You wrote the pamphlet *Leagues of Sovereignty*. Having that in my possession got me sent here! I want you to work with us. You read and write in . . . how many languages?" My enthusiasm flows out, which might drive him away.

"Seven. Six Rodentian, and that silly human one Canadian English. It's the funniest of them all except for Chipmunchian."

"Brother Golden-mantled ground squirrel, I would love to have you with us," I offer to him.

"In my language, I am a *zlatnoy tchshkishnoy tlesky squierlyterr*."

"So . . . in, Brother Squierlyterr, or out?"

"In, *tkerchshchiktsekkhquerkshertiquerk*!" he responds, with what I think is a whistle-filled Squirrelian obscenity.


Spunky and I met each other on the gold troughs far from the feeding troughs of the Inner Union elite. Here in the Yukon, north of our homes in the Rockies, we had no reason to fear death, because it was similar to what our wild cousins experienced. Death could come at any time. Any second. So Spunky, Soprano, an ever-changing cast of guest stars, and I would show up to talk around the stove in the warming tent, or out by a bonfire under the stars. We would squeak about faith, politics, philosophy, quantum physics, and the chicanery brought on by the ignorant antirodents who still held to species-ist notions.

One pine-scented night in between shifts on the troughs, we sit around the fire under the clear sky overhead. Others had been with us, but now we're all alone by the fire, except for the microphones nearby. Since we can die at any moment, we give ourselves the luxury of squeaking out authentically, without restraint. In the glow and warmth of the fire, I, Fearless the Shrie, huddle together with Soprano the Chipmunk, and Spunky the Golden-mantled ground squirrel to chew the fat and gnaw on a stick. And to gnaw on life's eternal questions. The roaring fire illuminates our cadaverous countenances, swaddled in quilted wool work jackets and coverings made from Dinosaur socks. Even though fire by its nature instills fear into us animals, its warmth provides comfort. Now we don't fear it at all. At least not here in the colony.

"Who could imagine all the spies in your midst? I, Spunky Kcherkcherktesherk, am an enemy because I believe in the power of community. Because our co-ops defend themselves against your RLA. We fight your fighters because you fight us! And I got news for you, rats! Most of the fighters in your RLA don't want to fight against us! I've smelled some of them working with us in our communities, and I'll whistle it to you: They're some of the biggest contributors we have." Spunky gets animated when he defends the Co-operative Leagues. I've read his work. That's why I'm here, to some degree. That and the fact that I pose a challenge to Steely's ego.

The co-ops are self-contained, self-owned, and self-regulated communities with their own means of production. They grow their own food, make their own products, and sell them in a responsible market within their self-contained economies. They use several commodities as currency. Steely has collectivized the commodities, so that growing them has to meet the approval of the planning boards. But in the co-ops, each lishek of rodents chooses what they will produce.

Peektah the house mouse scurries into our circle, dragging a twig in his mouth, then gnaws on it. Soprano leans over to him.

"We're bringing peace to the northern Rockies," Soprano chirps to the mouse through the cracking sound of the mouse's gnawing. The mouse puts down his twig.

"I want to thank you all for including me in your circle. I never had that anywhere else." The mouse's gratitude brings us a good feeling that we're doing something right. "I don't believe in a god or anything like that, but what we do here is more true spirituality than anything I saw in the church I grew up in."

We all thank him for his gratitude then Soprano offers up, "You grew up in a church?"

"Of course," answers the church mouse. "We used to steal the heavenly host and then we washed him down with the wine. It was delicious."

"But did you meet the Big Bunny and his dear sweet mother?" asks Soprano.

"No, can't say I did."

The mouse quiets himself, then I jump into this conversation. "As if the divine has to be a rabbit."

"But who are you to say what the divine looks like?" Soprano shrieks with whistling vitriol.

I spit out, "I was just asking whether we can know the Big Divine. That would be an insult to the whole goddess concept, wouldn't it?"

"I don't know anymore. I pursued faith my whole life. It's become the most upsetting thing at times," answers Soprano.

"Did you ever actually squat muzzle to muzzle with the Big Bunny?" I ask.

"No."

"Why not?" I shriek, then I check my Shrie spleen.

"You can't!" Soprano counter attacks.

The envy Soprano has toward me now comes to a head. I do the most spiritual thing I can think of.

"Brother chipmunk. I don't want this to become a religious war. Please, let's agree to disagree," I offer.

"But why is it you claim to have seen the Big Bunny when you're not even a Rabbitarian. I've served him all the days of my life . . . and he hasn't shown himself to *me*?"

As if I can answer that one.

Blacksnake scurries up to the fire with a tobacco pouch slung over his back filled with dried mushrooms and ergot fungus from wild oat ears. He settles in and passes a mushroom top to me.

"What if it's both? That's how I was raised," offers Blacksnake.

Spunky points out, "But what if the divine is in our midst? I'm here in this camp because I work with both Union and Co-operative League rejects. And the Union won't let me come back."

"A Co-op League brother!" chirps Soprano. "I never knew that about you. Which League?"

"The Banff Squirrel and Wood Chuck League. Local 933 Chee."

"The Arboreal Workers League. Number Thirteen. One of the originals," Soprano shares.

"We have a lot of siblings in here."

Peektah Ricotta enjoys a chew of firewood. He perks up his ears to listen to the air space above the other four. "Brothers! I see them. And I can hear them even better!"

"What do you see, brother mouse?" I ask.

The church mouse shares, "Flickering white tongues of fire above your heads . . . and there's a white rabbit!"

"Would you pass the ergot fungus and the 'shrooms, please?' asks Spunky.

"No! She's above us. The flames come from her," adds the mouse.

I feel an intuitive thought, coming from someone else, a voice drifting on the cold, biting breeze. "The power to heal your trauma is in your own paws. But you'll never heal alone."

"Can you describe the white rabbit?" I ask.

"She's taller than any of us. And she has some heavy cloth thing over her shoulders.

Some color I never seen before. And she has roses around her ears. She just talked to you, Fearless."

I drop the pouch as I stare at the mouse. "What did she squeak?"

"The power to heal is in your paws . . . But it is within us, that's what I sense."

I pick up the pouch and take out an oat berry with ergot on it, sniff it, and put it back. Something inside me senses I won't need hallucinogens ever again. Then I add my view. "I can agree with the 'within us' part. We're tragically alone if we don't have a larger group of people around us to function."

A chunk of dried mushroom come past the mouse. He nibbles on it, then shares his perspective. "I wouldn't believe this if you hadn't talked about this. I saw it for myself . . . that's the part that gets me."

"How do you know this isn't from Devil Kitty?" asks Blacksnake.

"Would Devil Kitty put white lights above our heads?" asks the mouse.

"Uh, yeah. He's the Great Deceiver. Get you to believe

he's Nature herself with the wrinkle of his almost-human whiskers."

"Is it because we need an antithesis to every thesis that you have your Devil Kitty idea?" I ask.

"Nature versus Devil Kitty. Rodentia versus humanity and humanistic thinkers in our midst. Protagonists and antagonist. The never-ending story of life," muses the mouse.

Soprano asks, "And the resolution is . . . ?"

Cappuccino scurries up to the bonfire, dressed in the wool sock with her colony number on the side. She keeps her head warm with a cat-fur hat with the big ear flaps flopping on each side of her head. She's never timid when we chew the fat. "Perhaps I can answer it best this way, brother chipmunk. The thesis states the purpose of the protagonist. The antithesis negates the purpose. So that negation becomes the purpose of the antagonist. The resolution negates the negation. But, as our glorious and ever-magnificent Big Cheese stated in his report to that plenum where we lost the rest of our natural liberties, 'The negation of the negation cancels itself out. It's simple arithmetic. Therefore, there is no negation of the negation. Synthesis is an unfulfillable wish. All life revolves around the eternal conflict, for the sheer purpose of conflict. Thesis and negation of the thesis. Conflict and war are the natural and everlasting course of the great reality of the here and now.' Pup! I can't believe I'd remember all that!"

The four of us fall silent at this horrible possibility of perpetual war and never-ending conflict. The crackling of the fire accepts the whistling wind as accompaniment, as stillness calms our souls. Gnawing sounds join that natural orchestra.

I stand up. "Would anyone like to synthesize with me over a cup of pine tea?"

"I would. And I have a drop of honey I can add," mentions Cappuccino.

"I can get more twigs for the fire," contributes Soprano.

"I can haul in some pine needles," adds Peektah.

"Let me build the fire up. I'm good at burning things," Blacksnake states eagerly.

I start us off with, "You see, siblings. In our synthesis, we negate our infallible leader's negation."

Later, over a steaming tin can of steeped pine needle tea containing wild berries and Cappuccino's honey, the discussion gets animated again. As it always does.

"Last week I didn't squeak faith in a higher power leads to irresponsibility. But I won't surrender myself to blind faith in magical thinking," I chirp at Soprano, the stalwart of the Rabbitarian faith.

"And isn't Spunky's faith in community a blind faith as well?" he counters.

"Communalism isn't a faith at all," responds Spunky. "The co-ops are an economic construct."

Soprano gnaws on the stump he's squatting on. "Then maybe you have faith in silver and gold," responds the striped squirrel.

"But it isn't a faith. It's a means of survival through social and communal participation."

"And who owns the means of production?" I inquire.

"The community," Spunky replies.

"How big is this community?" asks Cappuccino.

"We combine several hordes and shops together within our communities," he answers.

While Soprano finishes his gnaw, he has an epiphany. "You need a faith-based friendly group," offers the chipmunk in his heavy Chipmunchian accent.

Spunky responds, "We have no specific faith. It isn't about faith."

"Then are you all atheists?" Peektah the church mouse inquires.

"We have all faiths. Rabbitarians as yourself. Tree-hugging squirrels. Seems like every creek and river has its altar set up by beavers and muskrats. Earth worshipers, too."

"But whose faith is the true faith?" asks Blacksnake.

Cappuccino closes the argument with, "In my world view, there's just one divine. We all sense it in our own way."

After a long pause and more gnawing, I break the silence. "We got off track on religion when all I wanted to hear about were the co-ops."

"Maybe it's all interrelated," Spunky adds. And I think that explains it.

"What you Leagues talk about is exactly what I envisioned for our Union," I add.

"It's what comes naturally, Brother Fearless," whistles the Golden-mantled ground squirrel.

"We were meant to meet at this moment," adds Soprano, cheerfully flicking his bushy striped tail, regaining some of its pre-colonial luster.


"Make sure no one's going to squeal on us!" Blacksnake commands, as we gather around a fire in barracks fourteen. Gone are the old gangster elements that used this hovel as a house of prostitution and exploitation. Now, a new collection of khyazh stay here, yet the memories of horror linger in the resonance of the walls.

I stand up and sniff the air. "I feel the horror of this place is still here. Let's not be cowed by it."

"I ain't cowed," Blacksnake hisses. "But the walls have noses."

"What can they do to us? They could just shoot us. We're turning away from this nightmare system your AREU created," whistles Spunky.

"We didn't create it!" I chirp, "This isn't the real AREU. Hey, you were AREU! You cluck like you had nothing to do with what's happened to us!"

Spunky can't respond to that.

Through a small hole in between the walls, the house mouse Peektah Ricotta and Soprano squeeze in to join us. Soprano darts over to the fire. "We're late, we know. But we're being 'humaned' out by one of the Black Cats."

Blacksnake bristles up at this.

"Let's have a fair hearing on this one," I throw out.

Peektah Ricotta steps into the horrible atmosphere of the barracks. "I get a ringside seat into the central office's cat scat. I've been hiding in a hole under Pond Scum's office. There's only one Shrie singing to them."

The metal door gives off a tinny rattle, then swings open.

"Come on, rats! Get in there! Put 'em against the wall!" In come RLA fighters, scampering in with machine guns on their backs. Belch, now Senior Guard Belch, follows them in, pulls his weapon down into his paws, and whistles. The fighters form a semicircle. And so do we.

"Listen up, you thorned maggots on a pile of dog scat! Who is the thorned maggot who's been teaching *Shries how to read?*" My introduction to this scat hole taught me not to answer back to Belch. "Well, who?" he shrieks, like an insecure pup.

The tension fills the barracks, awakening the trauma in the walls. I gnaw on a big twig. Belch approaches me, then sniffs me out to intimidate me.

Commandant Pond Scum scurries in, followed by an entourage of colony officials. He draws out his slow scurry around the semicircle, sniffing as many of us as he can. Time draws to a phlegmatic drip. The commandant likes this power trip. And as the capstone of this hierarchy, he will do what it takes to break any challenge to his position.

The verbal standoff will be won by the one who remains silent. The first o squeak loses. The silence takes center stage in this symphony of power structure, accompanied only by a gentle breeze from outside and the gnawing sound of our siblings, doing what comes naturally for our species. They have the machine guns and the legal authority. We have each other, and a deep, strong craving for reality. Stalemate.

After what seems to be a ninety-month lifespan, Group Leader Pork-Rot throws in the towel to the ring of silence. "Why are you all here?" he begs to question. "One at a time, only! And only after I, or the commandant, ask you! Understand?"

"Sir, yes, colony commandant, sir!" we all squeal. A fighter pulls a stick out of the paws of a khyazh, then gnaws on it, leaving the sibling to sniff around for something else.

Pond Scum bristles up as he stands before Cappuccino. "You stink familiar. Who are you?"

"Cappu . . . I mean, Dah . . ."

"Address me properly, you sack of scat!" shrieks Pond Scum.

"Sir! Colony commandant, Dah 697, sir!"

"Oh, yeah! I remember now. You're a great thorn!" Pond Scum sniffs the air around himself. I try to avoid eye contact, but he sniffs my way, then steps up to me. A guard steps up to me as well, sniffing my fur.

"Sir! Colony commandant! This one stinks like Shay 383," squeals the guard. The camp commandant approaches me.

"Shay 383! You're the one teaching these other Jeemsh how to read and write! Isn't that so?" shrieks the rat.

"Sir! Colony commandant! I only wanted to end the violence, sir!"

"What violence?" chirps Pond Scum. "All I smell around me is we rodents acting naturally!" He steps away then squats in the middle of the barracks. "I, Colony Commandant Light-Bearer Pond Scum, hereby order the following to the white box! Shay 383, Chee 417, that's Chee 417 . . ." After the list is read off, Cappuccino, Blacksnake, Soprano, and a few others join me on a march to the white boxes, guarded by eighty RexCom fighters and twenty-four guard ferrets. I feel better already.

## Chapter Twenty-Four

# CAT CLAW

Cat Claw watches reports from the Midworst on a liberated computer monitor. Our siblings bite tail in the Dinosaurs' great American heartburn! Thirteen million of the beasts sent into hovelessness, with neither food nor heat, exacerbated by the incredible minus twenty-three–degree temperature. No fuel, no nothing! And the Dinosaur Army, with both its regular and militia forces, paramilitary elements, and not to mention the armed security companies taking over the security duties, treat the hoveless like pests. Vermin. Thirteen million emaciated, broken, and completely traumatized varmints on two legs, wandering aimlessly across a terrain devoid of sustenance. Once upon a time they were all awaiting a zombie apocalypse. Now they're the zombies.

The command post buzzes with animated hope. The location is itself a liberated cargo container buried under earth and rubble, connected to about fifteen others, and modulated for multiple uses. This cargo container holds three floors of space used by different elements of the intelligence units. This big space has a huge liberated fifty-four–inch television monitor at one end, and in front of it nine cubicles buzz with activity, each with its requisite laptop, earphones, cell phones, and digital tablets too heavy to pick up.

Intelligence teams in front of the screens squabble about what to research next. Or play computer games, considered impromptu training by most. Bushy tails and bright eyes squat before the blue glow of the screens. RexCom's monopoly on liberated technology is a thing of the past.

Cat Claw casts myopic eyes on a liberated computer monitor. On the screen, the view from a cloned drone appears as a building full of Dinosaur security near a FEMA camp explodes. The team in front of the monitor explodes with joyful shrieks of "Rhu Ski Chew!"

The screen changes to a modular building, not unlike this cargo container. Standard Ratsqueak letters appear on the screen with the description of a mobile command post for Dinosaur drones. Inside, the enemy targets us. Just like we're targeting them. The Dinosaurs use around eighty-nine of their species to operate just one of the warbirds. (We take more. Can't tell you how many. If I did, I'd have to gnaw you to death.) Over this command post one of ours releases a laser-guided bomb cloned from purloined samples. The target, with its dozen or so crew sitting in comfortable chairs, watching a similar view on their monitors through better human eyes, peacefully sits. A speedy streak of gray scampers to the modular unit, then the screen turns bright gray for a blink of a cricket's eye, giving way to the familiar black-and-white ball of fire on the ground.

From the cubicle next door, a senior officer in a green

and dark blue uniform of the RLAAP calls to my one-time assistant.

"Now, Executive Commissar Cat Claw. Our mobile Squeaky unit will take over controls of the three drones."

"Three more of theirs in our hands. Great work, comrades." offers Cat Claw.

The screen goes blank. Then the power shuts off. Screeches pierce the space, then the lights come back up. A team of RexCom officials scampers into the command space. One, a fox squirrel with a cardboard tube the size of a cigarette in his jaw, leads the team to perch itself under the big monitor. All wear the black kepi, so much different than the natural-colored headgear of the units behind monitors. The fox squirrel flicks his bushy tail in excitement, obviously enjoying his work. He drops the tube and pulls out a piece of paper.

"By executive order of the Big Cheese, all information in Nature is hereby considered to fall under the heading of 'an essential commodity,' as stated in the doctrine of War Collectivism. All electronic information and intelligence will be placed under the control of the new Central Information Administration. You will all relinquish your command and your posts to the RexCom officials coming to assume the duties of surveillance."

The RexCom officials push their way into the command space. Cat Claw sniffs the air, bristling up his fur, dropping his jaw slightly. The screens reappear showcasing guinea pig Volunteers for Victory squatting in the desert. The characteristic flash of a nuclear blast envelopes the screen.

"Comrades. Are you all proficient enough to fulfill this task?" hisses Cat Claw.

"What?" guffaws the squirrel in his Squirrelian accent. "You're all relieved. We don't answer to any of you. Dismissed!"

Over two million humans lie dead across the landscape of what they knew as North America. Along the Rio Grande, as the humans call that river; in Lah; Dinosaur Universal City that they named "Dee See;" wherever they congregate, there they lie. Living humans sit in the rubble across the Midworst, frozen from the several Arctic surges that thrashed the central northern hemisphere. Far more are going to join them over the next several months, all the way until their harvesttime. We expected them to collapse by now, but they haven't.

In Ann Arbor, outside of liberated Detroit, the 39th RLA Field Army fights with the last few thousand of its fearless and cunning fighters. Starting with a force of over 139,000 fighters, officers, and an inspiring cadre of political officers and commanders, the several thousand who haven't been hit hold ground as a new field army scurries in to replace them. The 13th RLA isn't a RexCom unit. RLA fights from the inside! Attacks from the rear! An RLA field army absorbs the landscape under its feet, then pours out into the landscape as the humans return. The only ones RexCom attacks in the rear are our RLA units.

Not far away, our brave United Lake Erie Irregulars stand by their antihuman guns and the ever-present multiple rocket batteries. This collection of local and regional forces democratizes the Rodentian war effort as a partisan army loosely associated with our Union. Fighting off a counterattack from over three thousand Dinosaur army fighters, they continue to pound positions in Canton, Ohio, as the Dinosaurs encircle their position.

To the west of the fighting, a FEMA camp formerly a collection of box stores smolders after the eight thousand inmates held there by the Dinosaur army rioted, prodded along by our drone strike against their army's bivouacs. All

the fluoride in their drinking water couldn't keep them docile
enough, apparently. And some of the soldiers sympathize with
the inmates. They open the gates and lead the refugees out to
freedom, so they can again roam free. The glue of humanity's
civilization fails, allowing chaos to be our ally.

Cat Claw scampers through an unfamiliar old sewer line that
runs under the liberated section of his new home, the Five
Burrows. With its mean sewers and humans who will never
give the city up, Cat Claw stays on the alert. The Dzumbani
here pride themselves on cat wrestling, and all their resulting
scars. And the river of beer drank and pissed out by the siblings here. Nature, think of the species-riots in this town! One
lone Shrie against a gang of Dzumies?

   Without purpose, life gets confusing. Time gets wasted.
One drifts, being seen as a parasite on the body politic of the
Union. Cat Claw scurries around aimlessly after given his dis-
charge from the Union. His RLA credentials still stand strong,
but the rats he knows have been muzzled out by RexCom
as traitors and spies. And without a specific function in the
machinery of state, Cat Claw will face the damning charge of
being an antinatural bump on a log, a slacker. Cat Claw served
the RLA against rebellious Co-operative League elements,
taking bird shot in his thigh. He still has the scar under his fur.
Nobody he squeaked with disagreed with the Co-op Leagues.
Now, this task of exterminating humanity will require every
rodent to participate. But they're disappearing. And we know
why.

   And don't forget the drunken rodents either. (Of course,
we had the "soused mouse disease" back in the Rockies as

well.) Cat Claw moves past several drunken rats by an aluminum beer can. The dipsomaniac siblings gnaw their way into their own demise as they bite into that can. Scampering past them, he scurries along a drunken mouse lying on its back, warbling out some slurred songs of his fathers, a sad caricature of his species, so crafty in verse and the spoken word, yet stewed to the gills like a fish *u riblijoj čorbi*.

"Can you spare some cheddar, me brother?" he squeaks at Cat Claw. "Can you spare some cheddar, me bro . . . me bro . . . me bro?"

"I ain't your bro!" Cat Claw shrieks back. He bristles up at the mouthy little mouse.

"Go ahead! Do me in! I don't want to live anymore! This planet is a sssssstinkin' and sssssstinkin' an' did I squeak, sssssstinkin'?"

"Oh? And what's so stinking about it?" Cat Claw demands.

"It's a real stinking thorned ass ol' world when a few stinking rats with human hearts own all the stuff the rest of us need so bad. It's a . . . its's a real . . . real . . . sssssstinkin' world when we have to stick our snouts up you bureaucrats' asses to get a Nature-damned oat groat . . . oat groat . . . *oat grrr* . . . *oat*!"

Cat Claw pounces on the mouse then freezes in his tracks. Memories of burning mouse hovels fill his soul. His conscience pulls him back, like a leash on a dog that can't correct itself.

"My dear sousey mousy. I wish you would find a solution to your grave troubles with sobriety."

As my one-time aid scurries away, the little dipsomaniac of a mouse stands proud and sure with a clear and present last statement, "I'll have that solution when beer flows freely down the gutter as a river of milk churns itself into butter!"

Down the gutter a ways, Cat Claw smells a familiar spot. Up the wall he goes, using those fine climbing skills all of us rats take pride in. On the way to his hovel, he smells a rat. And a house mouse. Both well fed, well hydrated, well dressed. Clean brothers. Neither is female. Cat Claw comes to the entrance.

"Commissar Cat Claw, I presume." The voice is mousy, strong, focused. The three sniff the air, as the Dzumban next to the mouse chews on some wiring.

"What do you two want?"

The wiring drops, creating a tiny click from impact on the concrete below. In a liberated basement of an office building filled with monitors and giant television screens, panels with over four thousand RexCom operatives play surveillance roulette by listening in on conversations and Nature knows what else. One of them switches channels after losing the sound from the squeaker under Cat Claw's belly.

"There. You can have your privacy back," clucks the Dzumban.

"Brother, you may not remember me, but we've worked together in the Union," squeaks the mouse in his soft yet firm no-nonsense Mousian accent, so different than a field mouse's. "My name is Cheesy Cornpuff."

"Don't remember."

"And my name is Duck Bill," adds the Dzumban.

The mouse takes charge, leading the conversation. "We're here to help you." This gets a suspicious response from Cat Claw. "You've been close to our great Brother Fearless from the western mountains. We want to let you know he's very much alive and we want to keep it that way."

"So?"

The two rodents sniff the air, listen around, and then turn to Cat Claw.

"There's hope for the Union, brother," confides the mouse.

"You can serve our order better than you can imagine," adds the rat.

These two and Fearless aren't the only AREU member that's ever been a little disappointed with the new smell of leadership in Universal City. Here and there, across the rodentscape, and in the highest echelon of power within the Union comes a loosely knit collection of dissenters from both Union members and the remaining leaders of the RLA. They find each other, ever-hypervigilant to the intrigue of RexCom. Which has its own dissenters as well, since the good, decent rodents in RexCom get purged and colonized the same as everyone else.


Meanwhile, back in the death camp . . .

"Why are you here?" I ask Slinky Mink, a gopher from the prairie who made it all the way to Universal City, in service to our Union, now a khyazh.

The gopher, with the insecurity that comes with a new environment, sniffs around, then gets close to me, sharing his forbidden secret. "I'll tell you, Brother Shay 383. At the last plenum . . . Comrade GenSec Steely stood up and before he gave his squeak, he started with . . . well, he thought it was funny. I still don't get it."

"What was it?"

"He asks . . . 'What comes between me and my Calvin Klein's?' And I whistled out, 'I don't know! What does come between you and Calvin Klein . . . ?'"

"And?"

"My whole tribe was volunteered for 'Victory.' And I was sent here for twenty months."

Back at the Plenary Conference, Steely dominates the assembly hall floor. He stands before the four hundred or so dignified political wonks of the Inner Union's service structure when he delivers this joke.

"Let Comrade Steely offer it again. What comes between me and my Calvin Klein's?" Silence fills the assembly hall in anticipation. "That's right. Nothing."

The silence continues, until Steely gets agitated from the dead air. Then he becomes stern, businesslike. "Alright, we need . . ." The Great Hall erupts in stilted and forced laughter. Rodents of every species contributes their whistles, shrieks, and clucks.

"That's the greatest humor we ever appreciated!" shrieks a pack rat. The others join in.

Steely silences them all and continues.

"Was that too dated?" he inquires.

"No, no, no, no . . ." shouts the assembly.

So, back to us, the frozen, starving, colonized siblings. I rack my big-ass brain the size of a pecan shell over this offense by the good brother, then I ask that emaciated gopher another question. "Was there a punch line?"


Back in that other universe, in another abandoned mansion in the Hamptons, Steely and his partner, Madam Snaketooth, host another party. Sunrise approaches. As most of the guests lie around in undignified drunken positions, crews of RexCom photographers and video crews with cameras made from re-manufactured cell phones encourage inebriated guests to take embarrassing selfies that will show up in the organs of Union information. The house mouse Cat Claw knows as Cheesy sits by a passed out girl prairie dog, as four violent squirrels in messed-up uniforms of the RLA general staff take turns on her. Probably the only squirrels left on staff. And at this moment, if Cheesy gets his way, these drunken scum will be in the colonies as well. After the latest purges, they could be the general staff over the hundreds of millions of RLA fighters. The mouse's ears scan the room. By the bar on the other side of the one-time reading room, the Dzumban who introduced himself as Duck Bill does the same.

Steely crawls onto a pile of old Dinosaur books, gigantic things that make a wonderful platform. Standing up on his hind legs, he whistles like a gopher calling the soused party's attention. "The night grows old, my siblings. And your good Comrade Steely would hate to mix business with pleasure, but . . . let's play 'Catch the Traitors!'" The mouse and the Dzumban aren't amused. Nor ashamed. "I know, there's always a possibility . . . that you are all traitors!"

Steely leaves the platform to scurry slowly and deliberately among the drunken and less inebriated. He makes it to Cheesy, whose steely beady eyes won't flinch.

"And . . . I understand that some of the Inner Union members would like to begin the Post–Big Cheese Era early. You, oh brave comrade mouse, wouldn't happen to know anything about that, would you?" Steely's attempt at intimidating the steely-eyed mouse fails. "You know, brother, when you get a human around animals, after a while, the human loses all fear of them."

"I have nothing to fear, Comrade Steely. You, comrade, are Rodentia's husband!" the mouse squeaks with iron testicles and steel nerves.

Steely softens his stance. "Thank you, comrade . . . I don't believe I ever learned your name."

"Comrade Senior Commissar Catfight Romano, Comrade Steely." The mouse uses his real name and position, which gains the Big Cheese's trust.

"Perhaps, my mousy friend, I'll be safe with you in the capstone."

"Yes, sir, Comrade Steely."

## Chapter Twenty-Five

# NATURE IS A WIDOW

In Factory 319, the largest assembly plant of the Comrade Chirpy Ruskachew Memorial Manufacturing Complex, a most tragic of mornings unfolds just before the third shift comes on to work. The music on the PA system broadcasting through scrubbed up, old, evaporated milk cans fills the environment with a predictably tinny "whee-whee" sound that might actually be electronic, might be live. Abruptly, it fades to silence. After a few seconds, a sad choir of rodents sings a liberated choral adaptation of *Adagio for Strings* by Tomaso Albinoni. Sung as a lament, the music demands the attention of both crews. The shop steward steps into the main work area and gets on a table after the machinery comes to a complete stop. The chief director of the factory stands next to him with a black megaphone made out of a tin can, emblazoned with the white emblem of the Union in a white circle. The shop steward takes it into his paw and tries to speak through tears.

"Comrades! Siblings! Nature is a . . ." and he collapses in wet, tearful sorrow. The director takes the megaphone, his fur-covered face getting soggy.

"Comrades. This morning, something terrible has happened to our . . ." the director crawls into a fury fetal position, cut down in his own pain.

"What is it!" comes a voice from the assembly. The director tries again.

"Big Cheese . . ." More grief immobilizes him.

"Excuse me, comrades," interjects a Shrie in a leather apron. "Is Big Cheese, how should I say . . . under the weather a little?"

Another stands up on a workbench. "More than a little, I would guess . . . I'm just saying . . . nothing too bad I . . ." He is cut off by the weeping of the two in charge.

A female gopher with a black bandana around her head hops up to the table. She takes the megaphone out of the paw of the director, as Albinoni continues in the background.

"Don't tell us he resigned?" As she drops the megaphone from her muzzle, she too becomes overcome by emotion.

A chubby brown rat in a dark gray dzash and workers' hat squeaks out, "Is our most righteous leader for whom all Nature counts it a privilege to . . ." then is cut short by a squirrel, bright-eyed at the suspense.

"Comrade Steely didn't just stub his toe, I would gather," the squirrel inquires. His answer comes across the PA system, heard all across Rodentia. Wherever the technology grants it, the announcement begins.

"Dear comrades. Rodents, siblings in the order. All our species unite together . . . at this most tragic of moments . . . Nature is a widow! Every animal an orphan . . . That great rat, Comrade Dzo Dzugash Veeley, our beloved Comrade Steely has left us this morning . . ." *Dun-dun-dah*! Dramatic Chipmunk appears, standing up, turning his head to look us straight in the eye.

"This is the worst thing ever to happen to Nature," shrieks a house mouse dressed in laborers' bib overalls. She takes the megaphone. "Forgive us, our guiding light, our champion, the only rat worthy of the honorific 'Big Cheese.' For you are aromatic cheese. Pungent and comely. Better than gold."

The postmortem accolades flow like salmon upstream during spawning season. In every factory, on the train rides back home later that morning, in schools, and on the front lines, the news stuns the whole movement. Outside of Pittsburgh, the 2nd Armored Grenadier Division stops its advance on the outskirts of the city and conducts a collective mournful squeaking of grief. Some mice die of shock after hearing the news. Many don't want to believe such distressing news. No one dares express anything like joy or laughter. In Indiana, two rats are shot without warning by the local security apparatus for joking about Dinosaur sex after the news went forth.

As the nights follow, a steady stream of siblings flows throughout the Great Hall of Evolution, where Steely lies curled up on a cushion upon a liberated bed stand, dressed in his work dzash, as though he's going to get up and give us a speech, then write all evening. In that common rat's uniform, bathed and shampooed, his reflection in a mirror above the bier shows him in repose, with his profile easy to see and recognize. Roses around the bier give their therapeutic comfort to the grieving masses filing past. Between the grieving stream and the bier, cushions with magnifying glasses in front of them contain Steely's medals and accomplishments so that they can be seen easily. At each side, and throughout the hall along the walls, by columns and entryways, stand honor guards dressed in sharp, cleaned, and starched uniforms; the RLA in natural cotton uniforms; the RLAN in white sailor blouses, striped sailor shirts, and unbilled sailor caps trailing tassels behind them; and RLAAP fighters in gray tunics and black trousers, trimmed in white. All either hold the Type 80 assault rifle across their chests or hold in their front right paw the Type 79 rifle with black triangular pennants tied to the affixed bayonets.

The morning of the funeral, the body goes into an L-shaped building in front of Martyrs Field, where Rodentia's greatest heroes are interred in the garden's earth under the lawn. Each grave is covered with a rock the size of a pack of cigarettes, the names and deeds of the buried engraved into the stone. In the main entrance, Steely's body lies in state until all the eulogies are given, all the accolades proclaimed, all the affection, honest or contrived (mostly for show and self-protection), have been so eloquently spewed on both the living and the deceased. Then the pallbearers, the most trusted of the inner circle, as well as the most heroic of the RexCom fighters in their sharpest uniforms, bear the funerary cushion carrying the Big Cheese out of the building, down the steps, made passable with decorative plywood ramps, down to a paved pathway that leads to an auditorium nearby. The mass of rodents outside shed more tears, stampede, and kill hundreds of their siblings without breaking the slow cadence of the cortege.

At the auditorium, the body moves past as the GenSec's personal marching band and the Great Rodents' Opera per-form "Lachrymose" from *K. 626*, with completely rewritten lyrics in Standard Ratsqueak. Soldiers and siblings carry the flowers in their muzzles that accompany the cushion bearing the remains. Snaketooth, in utter despair, squealing in pain over her loss, is the last one permitted into the auditorium. Then the doors close on the "Amen." Yet *K. 626* continues till it finishes. And inside, behind the doors, a tile pulled from the masonry on the floor of the entry will be replaced with a new marble one in white, the simple engraving reading "Steely. The Big Cheese of the All Rodents Evolutionary Union, Year minus Six to Year Zero. All Honor to our Elder Statesrat." With some of the flowers and a collection of one-ounce bottles of liqueur liberated from an airport, the cushion descends slowly and reverently into its final resting place, so unlike the untold hundreds of millions of siblings dumped into ditches or allowed to rot and feed crows and desperate feral cats. The grave will have a clean garbage bag draped over it over a squared off section of cardboard between the elder statesrat and the green plastic covering. Within an hour, the memorial tile will be cemented in place and given a week to cure. And the Big Cheese will belong to the ages.

Chapter Twenty-Six

# THAW

Like small rivers of iced café au lait, muddy waters cascade under the railroad trestle a locomotive chugs over, festooned with black flags and banners, and emblazoned on the front with a cameo in copper of Grand Mother Nature leading the rodents. The smell of Doug fir and pine mingles with the smell of creosote amid the gentle, comforting roar of the runoff. The rhythm of the clanging metal keeps time with the rocking of the boxcars filled with RLA fighters and all the supplies for the colony.

We, the members of the salon, as I like to think of it, squat in whiteness as we pay the penance for our freethinking. I like the penalty, hey, I like being an irreverent bad rat! We get to meditate in silence for hours on end, wrestle with our inner demons, strengthen our chakras, come into contact with chakras we didn't even know we have. And I've been stretching and creating new yoga asanas. Being a bad rat is where it's at!

All good things must come to an end, which I think is complete cat scat, but I hear rattling at the door of my microwave oven turned prison cell and sanctuary. The door slowly swings open to reveal four RexCom guards with their black armbands and submachine guns.

"Shay 383! Come out of there!" shrieks the biggest guard, a Shrie with one ear ripped off. I creep out, then follow them outside into the cold. The other salon members join me as we follow our guards to the assembly point. Overhead, the morning light fills the sky, letting us know we'll be kept past our bedtime. The guards release us into the general population.

At the colony assembly point, all of us inmates stand at attention, bow to the bust of the late Big Cheese, and confess our transgressions one more time, asking for his mercy and forgiveness. Then we bow again and crouch down. I have forgotten what my transgressions are, so I make stuff up. They make up stuff about all of us, so I might just as well do the same. Commandant Pond Scum stands with his black Dixie Cup megaphone on the white-washed podium.

"Attention. Attention. Your attention, please! Listen to this most important message. We will begin a seven-night mourning period for the passing of our beloved . . . Big Cheese." Wiping away a big cheese-size tear, he pauses and takes a breath. "Our glorious leader, father of the Union . . ." I bite my tongue in disgust at this. ". . . husband of Nature . . . the only father I ever knew. Though he was so far away from us, I felt like he was closer to me than any family member I ever had. I came from a litter of nineteen pups. Poverty-stricken rats in a dump. We were my mother's second litter. She had two more. I think she had forty-one of us altogether. Thirty made it to adulthood. None of our fathers did." He wipes another tear away. "They were *SPERM DONORS*! But our father, the Big

Cheese, was my father! The . . . excuse me, *our* Big Cheese . . . was always there. He was a better rodent than most who I've ever known. I know he could be a hard tail, but cat gone it . . . we need a leader like that. We need a rat we can fear. We never had some ineffectual, soft-tailed rat of a boss. We had a true rat." In the distance, a locomotive's whistle pipes out in the morning air, catching everybody's attention.

Pond Scum puts the megaphone to his muzzle one more time. "I have nothing but contempt for those of you who stand against such a noble pup of the universe. I'm glad I became what I've become. I hope I'm the scourge in the paw of Big Cheese! May he always be bigger in death than he was in life."

We inmates crouch in wonder at this soliloquy. Pond Scum hands the megaphone to Pork-Rot, his new aide-de-camp. Pork-Rot addresses the crowd, weeping in cheepy sorrow.

"The Big Cheese, may he live in our hearts and souls forever and ever without end, passed away the eighth night post-vernal equinox, in the year Zero. He was surrounded by his beloved daughters, and those on his staff who he found most trustworthy." Pork-Rot wipes a tear away before it freezes on his face. "Our beloved Comrade Steely was mourning the tragic . . . but necessary and heroic loss of his beloved son Stink Bug who preceded him in death the week before, killed in combat by a sniper's bullet."

The armored train pulls into the railroad loading dock. All, including the bullying staff, stop to listen to the train, for it is a very long train, with four of the largest and most powerful types of locomotive pulling it.

Pond Scum turns back to the assembled inmates. "Pay Attention! There will be a seven-night mourning period, as of right now. For the next seven nights there will be complete silence on your part!" From the direction of the train, a detachment of the RLA unit scurries toward the assembly along the edge. Pond Scum points his muzzle their way, wrinkles his whiskers, and continues. "For the next seventy-two hours, you will be allowed only water. No work will be done. Every day you will bow to the sacred statue before you and say in unison, 'Most special Comrade Steely, without you, life itself is not worth living.'" Pond Scum again turns his attention to the army unit. "Now, before we dismiss, let us continue by singing the sacred hymn, 'For the Love of Comrade Steely.' At the sound of the tone, everybody." Pond Scum makes a tone. The whole camp sings the song, stretching it out to avoid contact with the approaching army unit.

The whole RLA 26th Independent Shock Brigade, a unit of 7,200 or so rodents, fully integrated and inclusive, started the journey from Utah two weeks ago. All but one were healthy, strong rodents. The unhealthy one, an antelope ground squirrel from Lake Tahoe, brought some uninvited guests with him. Their own pests, *Yersinia Pestis*, make their home in the bodies of two-thirds of the brigade right now, aboard this train.

Pond Scum calls his own unit of bodyguards. "Special lishek! Follow me! The rest of you . . . stay where you are! In complete silence!"

The unit of forty or so go with him to the locomotive. They stop at the window where the engineer drives the train.

"Fighter Sweetwater!" calls Pond Scum, to a RexCom pack rat. "Knock on the door."

The pack rat approaches the door below the window. He gnaws on it, then whistles up at the engineer room. The door swings open, causing a putrescent stench to pour out of the engineer compartment. He turns to the commandant.

"Go in!" commands Pond Scum.

The pack rat disappears. Pond Scum runs up to the opening, and as he crawls into the train, down from the roofs of
several cars come banners with the most dreaded image in the
rodent's heart. On each banner, a black circle around a white
disk contains the stylized black image of a flea on its back.
Where its eyes would be are two white x's.

"Plague train!" screams Pond Scum. The RexCom fighters
shriek in terror at the sight of RLA fighters wearing rubber
NBC suits and gray gas masks. They all scamper away from
the train out into the nearby grove of trees. The khyazh, so
well trained, squat in defeated submission, silently awaiting
orders. A rat wearing a gas mask opens a window to the lead
locomotive then pokes his head out. A door opens from the
third train car, and out scurries a detachment of RLA fighters
in gas masks and rubber suits. Dead rats and gophers drop out
of the opened hatch, all of them with the telltale lumps of
buboes on their bodies.

I stand up with Spunky by my side. We sniff the air toward the train, then in unison, we scurry to the open hatch. A
mouse tries to stop us.

"No, brother. You'll get us all killed!"

"What are you, comrade? A mouse or a man?" I bark at
him like a mountain shrew.

"He's right!" whistles a nearby gopher. I ignore them as I
scurry to the train. Spunky smells me moving, then joins me.
And Blacksnake comes up to do so as well. I sniff the air behind us, and smell Soprano joining us. But none of the others
move. They just squat in fear of RexCom retaliation. But far
away now, in the shadow of the trees as the sun rises, RexCom
shakes from fear of the pestilence.

"You'll need a medical corps rat to help you," I hear behind me. Sure enough, Cappuccino joins us, sniffing the air

around us and assessing the train as her whiskers vibrate. We come to the hatch under the engineer's window. The stench dissipates, sort of. Actually, it hangs in the air, as though it has a life of its own. Then the stench gives way a little with the scent of Peektah Ricotta coming to the forefront.

"You'll need me, brethren. As a mouse, I can't get the plague," he fearlessly offers.

"Anybody in there?" I shriek. A squeak muffled by gray rubber answers my question. Then a sibling appears, in full NBC gear.

"*Mumble-mumble- mumble-mumble,*" the sibling squeaks, not making any sense through all the protection. Each NBC suit has a layer of latex, then spun glass, then cotton, then more spun glass, then charcoal, then more spun glass, then polyester. And one more cotton body glove. Squeak through that and try to make sense! Everybody hates Nuclear, Biological, Chemical warfare training.

"May we come in?" I ask.

The mask comes off, revealing a girl prairie dog with big, pretty eyelashes.

"Stay out! You have no authorization!" squeals Pretty Lashes.

"Is it true that this is a plague train?"

"It is now. We are looking for the Shriedaygahbah, Fearless the Chairmouse!"

I creep up to her, sniffing her whiskers. "Did you say 'Fearless'?" I ask.

Pretty Lashes sniffs out my whiskers, then takes out a piece of the sock that Catnip held so dear to her soul. She puts it next to her muzzle, sniffing both the sock piece and me.

"Comrade Chairmouse Fearless. It smells like you."

Behind the rodents, another in an NBC suit scurries up

to us. Off comes the gray rubber gas mask with the tube attached, and when the whiskers vibrate again, the nose of the uncovered Shrie goes to work.

"Comrade Chairmouse Fearless. I would know your scent anywhere."

I sniff out the unmasked rat in the NBC suit and freeze into a defensive pose as his pheromone triggers a visceral response in me, throughout my whole body. "Cat Claw!"

"Brother. Comrade. I'm here to take you home."

"You were there!"

"Where?"

"The interrogation theater!" I shriek, my PTSD leaking out again. Cat Claw freezes with a "what?" visage on his muzzle. "You watched me betray my beloved. You spied on me the whole time!"

"Brother, your beloved is free," Cat Claw states with confidence.

"Don't lie to me you tail hole!" I shriek at him. I could kill him right now, with orgasmic pleasure. Then I let him have it. "Now I know . . ."

"No, brother . . ."

"Comrade! I am still your superior!" I squeal at him.

"Please forgive me, comrade."

"Why?" I chirp with such a low vocal fry that even a human can hear it. "For serving *it*?"

"Comrade?"

"I serve the Evolutionary Union! You serve that dead rat, that stinky human, that smelly human spoiled cheese, the Big Stinky Cheese! Shoot me now, I don't give a scat! I'm beyond hating Steely. I am now . . . *indifferent* to our failed, fallen leader. Possibly the best thing he ever did for us! Shoot me, you fool!

Bite me in the front! You've been back-biting me this whole time, haven't you?"

"Comrade Chairmouse, there's a new administration being formed as we squeak! A new night falls for all of us, brother. And we want you to be a part of it, Comrade Chairmouse."

"Trust him." Beneath all the rancor and trauma of the last weeks, a voice speaks to my solar chakra, and the words resonate. Just those two simple words.

Morgana Fairy Foot brings the biplane down onto the open snow by a rust-streaked Quonset hut, once abandoned by the Dinosaurs, now reclaimed as a hangar. Somewhere near liberated Denver, the throne of power over the Rocky Mountain Front, Fairy Foot sits in front of the upper wings in the glass enclosed cockpit of her biplane. She would search the whole planet to find me, her half-brother. And she has clout with the other rodents, who are all unaware of her fairy DNA. Through its power, she creates her own privileges with the rats she takes to the nest. Blood vengeance, position, and wild oats by the pound . . . with a squeak she gets what she came for. The Earth is her oyster; dominance, her pearl of great price. And with these events unfolding, she's going to get that brass ring, as the Dinosaurs say.

Meanwhile, back in the Bronx, Madam Snaketooth decorates the space around the sink that previously served as her bathtub, but is now the personal shrine to her fallen alpha tomcat. Dominating the space above the sink faucets, a black-and-white portrait of her beloved hangs as though suspended from

heaven, just slightly above the Earth. She sniffs the image of
Steely with reverence and utmost respect. Votive candles burn
around the sink, and in a brass dish light gray smoke shares its
fragrance of frankincense with the widow as it snakes its way
to the ceiling, the kundalini traveling up the spine of mourning
on its way to the crown chakra of dominance.

"Excuse me, Comrade Supreme Cultural Director." Snaketooth feels comfort in hearing that familiar voice.

"Comrade Supreme RexCom Director Pike!" she squeaks
with enthusiasm.

"Sister, RexCom has just been voted out of existence by
the Supreme Secretariat," he chirps, the religious fanatic losing
his failed faith. But he repents his sin and stands up tall and
solid.

The Madam straightens up her spine, allowing her fur to
bristle. "The Supreme Secretariat made the decision?"

"The Supreme Secretariat just voted themselves as the acting governing authority. And now they're creating an ad hoc
committee to create a new All Rodents International!"

"They're dismantling all of Comrade Steely's hard work,"
she chirps bitterly. The two take a moment to look into the
beady eyes of her beloved above the sink. Then she breaks
the moment of silence. "Well, don't just squat there, Nature
dammit! Help me!"

The unruffled Pike gnaws on the ceramic and metal edge
of the sink. Then he wiggles his whiskers in her direction. "We
aren't alone in all of this, Madam."

But I smell the arrival of spring on the train heading back
to Denver. The plague stench dissipates, blowing out the open
windows. Over the trestle the train goes, moving freely through
the rain's gentle sprinkle like runoff in the spring thaw.

## Chapter Twenty-Seven

# CULTURE SHOCK

I expected snow and ice in Denver. The beautiful spring destroyed my expectations, along with my blessings. I smell the budding vegetation in the air and hear a gentle breeze in the trees. The only wintery thing left is my khyazh uniform. So I go clad in nothing but the sunshine, the way Grand Mother Earth intended us to be.

The train ripples from the shock wave of momentum caused by colliding with the stationary. The violence shakes me out of a comforting sleep. I sniff the air around me, wiggling my whiskers, my antennae to the world around me. I hope I can get a good reason to lift myself out of the comfort of my nest, made from cardboard and chewed-up toilet paper. A squirrel in starched green parade dress scurries into my boxcar.

"Denver! Brothers, we're coming into the Denver station!

Get your stuff together!" whistles the squirrel. That's reason
enough.

Our arrival in Denver holds no celebration. The plague
flags sit rolled up in their storage spots somewhere in one of
the front railcars. The masks and rubber suits stand ready in
their bags to protect us from humanity's aggression. The survivors of the plague go about their duties, while we liberated
khyazh enjoy the ride back. Now, the big challenge will be
assimilating back into the world we once knew.

The sun shines on us as we scamper off the train and onto
the concrete siding. I left my khyazh clothes back on the train.
Or maybe on the siding in Alberta or somewhere. Anyway,
I feel the sunshine on my fur, as warm as my mother's love
for us pups. Hey, even nocturnal creatures need loving and
sunshine. And the fact that it's the setting sun means night
comes into its own station for us rats.

I make my way past sandbags and platoons of fresh young
pups in clean new field uniforms and full field gear. The smell
of plastic in the air brings to mind my service in the RLA. I
smell plastic and I immediately think of the little green army
men we use as unit markers in our war games.

"Fearless! Chairmouse Fearless Litzkachew!" The familiar
voice of my one-time aid and continual benefactor (maybe)
comes across the concrete. I wiggle my whiskers in the direction of his voice.

"Chairmouse Fearless!" whistles a squirrel from the same
direction. I can tell she's female by the resonance of her voice.

"What do you want?" I squeak back.

The two approach me, and after a quick sniff of each
other, I check Cat Claw out with my whiskers. "Comrade Cat
Claw." I ask, "Who's in charge of this town now?"

"The ad hoc committee," replies Cat Claw.

"Brother," whistles the squirrel, "We have a place for you to stay here in town."

"A cell, right?" I squeak suspiciously.

"Comrade, you're going to be rehabilitated by the ad hoc committee," Cat Claw states with confidence.

I'll believe it when I smell it.

The bright-eyed sister flicks her bushy tail with excitement. "Comrade Cat Claw. We have to go. They're expecting us," she insecurely states.

"Sister, don't worry about it. We're on our way. Comrade Fearless, would you please come with us?" Cat Claw and the squirrel head toward the dimming light of the front entrance. I follow. What else am I going to do?

We bounce around in a Bump 80. This one has a radio and three long antennae sticking out the roof. We stop, start, barrel down fast, then we slow down to a slug's crawl. Cat Claw gets all agitated, and the squirrel digs around a pile of papers like she's digging for her peanuts.

"We're here, Comrade Fearless. Follow me in. We're going to meet the Committee," Cat Claw throws at me as he gets his stuff together.

"What about my friends on the train?" I ask.

"Don't worry about them. We're providing for them, too," he answers.

The Bump stops. The right hatch swings open.

"Come on, Comrade Fearless," whistles the squirrel. I climb out the hatch and hop onto an asphalt road. The two rodents escort me through a door down into the open space of what had been a box store. Now its floor holds dirt and rubble as resistance against the expected nuclear strike. They lead me into a basement room with maps on the floor. The familiar smell of plastic army men comforts me.

Around the maps, our executive commanders in starched, clean uniforms confer with real commanders in filthy field uniforms. I'm still natural, and I feel insecure being with these rodents without some sort of uniform. I nip at the squirrel a little.

"Sister Squirrel? I need some type of uniform on me," I state.

"Comrade Fearless? I'm Senior Commander Nutty Klik-klchikkel," she replies. "Sir, we're going to get you settled in. Please be patient with us."

Sir! When did that word come to me last? I feel so out of place here, yet this is the environment I love! The two escorts move toward a bigger back room. Cat Claw sniffs in my direction.

"Comrade Chairmouse? Please, follow us," he requests. Politely. Now I feel detached from my surroundings, the respect shocks my system so.

We enter the back room where a group of our fellows mills around, sniffing the floor, gnawing on thick wires, and grooming themselves.

"Comrades!" squeals Cat Claw to the group as he stands up on his hind feet. "May I introduce to you all my former leader, who always treated me well, the chairmouse of the Ninth All Rodents International, Fearless Litzkachew!"

Everyone wiggles their whiskers, then whistles in honor to me.

A beaver joins us. "Comrade Chairmouse! Welcome back to Denver!"

I squat in shock and awe. "I feel kind of funny being naked."

"Who told you you're naked?" comes a squeak from the group. It's a sound I can recognize anywhere. But of course it couldn't be who it sounds like. No, Catnip died in the camps in some snuff video produced by the Steelian clique.

"Well, ain't I?" I respond.

"Let me smell that naked body of yours," comes the voice I feel love from—that feminine, woman-ratty voice my soul hungers for in the wee hours of the morning. I must be dreaming. She scurries, then scampers to me, squealing in a sad yet happy chirp. We collide and I smell that delicious Amazon Lady Rat. Then we sniff each other's tail holes to make sure we're not dreaming.

"Fearless!" shrieks my dear Catnip. I'm squeakless. She just purrs like a happy cat as we groom each other for the first time since our universes shattered after hearing the words, "You are under arrest!" I've never felt my soul so mixed up like it is at this moment.


Grass begins to sprout along the irrigation ditch behind the liberated apartment complex Catnip leads me to. I gently nip by her tail.

"Hey, ass-nipper," she growls, "What was that about?"

"Let's go swim in the ditch," I purr.

"It's cold!" she shrieks through her funny, peeping laughter.

"We'll warm it up!"

"Come on. We got hot water in my place."

"Is it far?" I ask.

"It's right over there! Come on!" She leads me into the apartment complex.

"Piss on the floor so they know who you are," she requests. And I oblige, trickling little drops all the way to her front door.

To get there, we crawl up the network of wood studs to the top floor, then take a staircase to the roof.

"Here's your new home, Fighting Ferret Soul," she purrs at the door. "Go in." I crawl through the chewed-out entry into a section of the attic divided by cardboard. "They're putting a bodega in the old room in the basement."

"What's a bodega?" I ask, feeling like an inexperienced field mouse.

"It's a shop where you can get all your basic stuff. All your food, at least. All major cities have them," she answers. "The communal bath is down on the third floor. And . . ." she bars the door from the inside, ". . . we're getting a security staff together. You ought to check it out. You can get to know the neighbors."

"Crime problem here?" I ask.

"Chipmunks," Catnip hisses. "They're all thieves."

"Anyone else to watch out for?"

"Not really," answers my special someone in her new love nest. "The neighbors are pack rats, and they're all hoarders. But maybe we can have a rummage sale."

Maybe I've been away too long, but Catnip seems like she's defected to suburbia. And that's where the enemy lives!

But then, I get thinking . . . is this an anomaly? Or are things just getting better?

"Catnip, this is such a nice life you've found. Does everybody live like this?" I ask.

She thoughtfully gnaws on a wood stud in the wall, then wiggles her whiskers my way. "I don't know."

After a nap, I wake up in the nest Catnip made for the two of us. She left a note for me, written on a coffee-stained sheet of human paper. On the sheet, a used but clean field uniform awaits me. I put on the clothes: a green shirt and those comfortable camouflage cutoffs everyone likes these days. And she left me a bottle cap with some food in it. I try it, and it's fishy. But I can go for fishy now. After finding an old teacup saucer with some fresh water in it, I feel ready to check out the world beyond Catnip's.

## Chapter Twenty-Eight

# DEVASTATION

I step outside the apartment into the comfortable spring night. A group of siblings in worn-out field uniforms mingle around a human dumpster. Graffiti written in several Rodentian languages partially covers the blue background and faded human graffiti on the dumpster. I scurry over to them, smelling their pheromones. A collection of Shries and Dzumbani. They sniff my way, vibrating their whiskers.

"Who are you?" one of their team squeaks.

"I'm your neighbor," I reply. "I smell unity among our species."

"We rats gotta stick together," a Shrie offers.

"Times are tough, Peepee," a Dzumban states.

Behind him, I hear two rats bantering.

"I still don't believe we've killed all the Dinosaurs in this town," squeaks one.

"We couldn't have. I fought in those caves the Dinosaurs have running under this city.

"They can live in there for *months*!" another answers.

A slender gopher joins their discussion. "Professionally squeaking, I've been in those tunnels. I killed three humans under this town with my recoilless rifle. I have to tell you all. I marvel at their handiwork. What humanity was capable of, with their machinery? Their excavatory intellect? Those Dinosaurs may be on the verge of extinction, but they sure can dig a hole in the ground!"

"I'd like to see them dig one in the sky," adds a Shrie.

The gopher gnaws on a metal soup can that hasn't been turned into an antihuman bomb, as of yet. "You fellahs call me 'the gophers' gopher' . . ."

"That's only when you bring us coffee," jokes a Dzumban to the peeps and giggles of the others.

"Call me a traitor and a soul criminal if you want. Send me to the colonies for what I'm about to whistle, but . . ."

"Cat scat!" chirps a Shrie, "there are no colonies."

I want to jump into this argument. "Brother Gopher," I whistle to him, "Please, finish."

"Who are you?" whistles the gopher, suspicious of me, the unknown rodent in their midst.

"I was Shay Taleka Kutitzeh Taleka until ten nights ago," I share. The group gets quiet. But I see contempt in the young doubting Shrie's countenance. I continue, "But my mama named me Fearless so I don't want to dishonor her. Brother Gopher, please, squeak your truth."

The gopher stands up, as though he were standing on the berm surrounding his hole. "I know this isn't what any of us wants to hear, but it's been a good hundred nights since Night

One. We're still up to our incisors with humans. May Nature rest her peace upon the dead soul of our departed Comrade Steely . . ."

"He was a human!" squeals the contempt-filled Shrie.

". . . Well," continues the gopher. "He promised us the last humans would be executed tonight, right on streaming video . . ."

The buzz of artillery ordnance from the human resisters interrupts the gopher's soliloquy. The earth shakes from its nearby impact. The group scampers for cover while I head back to the complex.


Several rounds fell near our home, but fortunately that first one was the only one to get close to us. Others fell to the east of us, and I heard gunfire in that direction for about an hour. Now that the fire has let up, I head back downtown. A free bus takes me past the old Botanic Gardens to a metropolitan train station, converted from the human sewer system. Still stinks in there. And humans live down in those sewer tunnels. Holdouts, sewer men who nauseate most rats.

I step off onto what smells like fresh concrete at Tivoli Station, under what had been a big bookstore on the campus of some Dinosaur university. Up a brand-new ramp leading into the bookstore, I scurry into an empty spot smelling vaguely familiar.

I feel the rumble of a steam train under my paws. A few siblings scurry out of the station below. From everyone's pheromones, I can tell it wasn't a fat winter in the least. Hardly more than ours in the Yukon. The mix of different urine scents confuses me as I try to get out onto the street outside.

A beaver in overalls scurries past me. He's easy to see, so I approach him.

"Excuse me, Mr. Beaver. Do you squeak Standard Ratsqueak?" I inquire.

The beaver whistles out, "No squeak Rattytalk."

I whistle out, in my best Beaverian, "Brother Beaver, I want the entrance . . ."

"Stop!" whistles the beaver, and I feel bona fide hatred in the whistle. "You sexist rat! What makes you think I'm male?"

I sniff her out. "Honestly, sister. I can't tell the difference."

"Nature, you're an ignorant pouch of cat scat! I am a *girl* beaver! There's no bone in my equipment!"

This is getting insane. "Please, which way to the station exit?" I whistle out. She slaps the floor with her tail, then scurries off.

I look for the brightest light with my 20/300 vision. A gopher in the black field uniform of some nearby regional militia scampers past me. I follow, trying not to judge what gender the gopher might be.

Fortunately, he or she is heading outside, so out we go. I scurry about, looking for any indication of how we're doing as a Union. I find a smattering of little kiosks along the street heading out of this one-time college campus, now community center. I scurry up to an outdoor kiosk. The aroma of starling stew fills the air. Over a nearby firepit, sparrows roast on a rotisserie made from an electric motor found . . . somewhere. Something small, anyway. I can't just scurry up to the proprietors. That would be suspicious. But I can smell. Listen. Pay attention to the thoughts squeaked and whistled out by the rodents in this gathering place.

At a nearby kiosk specializing in grilled vegetable pieces

and frog meat, a squabble breaks out between a squirrel in a natural cloth militia uniform and a Dzumban. While each hiss out insults in their own language, a chipmunk scampers up to the raw veggies awaiting cooking, and pockets them in his pouch. Or hers. Then the naturally striped thief scampers away. The kiosk owner, an emaciated porcupine, whines out a sad, apathetic call for help.

I scurry along, because, let's face it, I don't have the metabolism to go scampering after some evil chippy, who could easily have the heart and weapon to kill me for his veggies.

Then I notice something: the posters of the Big Cheese, looming over us all. Before I was arrested, they dominated the backdrop of the urban thoroughfares. Now they droop down, weathered beyond repair, some covered by new posters plastered over, others defaced with graffiti.

And the constant sounds from the broadcast squeakers with their microphones and two big ears sticking out of their round black bodies take up no space in the soundscape. I think to myself as I wander back to the station, "Fearless, ol' buddy. This is a power vacuum. If you don't fill it somehow, someone else will. Just like our glorious leader Steely." A luna moth flicks its wings as it flies above me, and I feel the ripple in the air as it does so. Maybe a butterfly can flap its wings in Denver and cause a landslide in Universal City two months later.

"I'm no butterfly! I'm a luna moth!"

I just received in my mind this thought from the luna moth. "I didn't say you were!" I squeak out loud to the space above my head. Then I notice: It's empty space.

## Chapter Twenty-Nine

# GATHERING OF SAGES

O ver the Rockies, early morning light just barely comes halfway across the navy blue sky. I'm back over near the Botanic Gardens in what the enemy named Cheeseman Park. In the distance a rototiller plows the former park's lawn for garden space. Hopeful for bigger dinners in the future.

I search the new Executive Command Post Central Office for Cat Claw. I smell his pheromone in the tunnel so he must be close. It's not an old aroma. Downstairs in the basement I find a large, open space with padded dividers stacked up on one side of a wall. Hanging over the room are fluorescent lights blazing their unnatural light into the space. I don't want to be under those evil lights. No healthy rat would. My one-time aid, dressed in a starched dzash jacket, scampers past me then stops to sniff me out.

"Comrade Cat Claw . . . how do you want me to address you?" I ask.

"Comrade Fearless! Please, address me as Comrade Cat Claw. I'm glad you're here, because I have to go to Universal City and I want you to accompany me."

I'm stunned. This is what I want. And I'm getting it. My ratty head spins at the unlikelihood of such good fortune. "How long before we go?"

"Thirty-six hours. I got to get ready," Cat Claw chirps out, then moves away.

I call out to him, "I want to bring some people along!"

He doesn't hear me, and he has big ears.

I have no idea where my mates from hell are. For all I know, Soprano got himself and his whole family sent back to prison. We brought the whole incarcerated family of chipmunks back here from the colony. But who knows where they are now? Cappuccino disappeared on me, again. Like she did the night I met her. Blacksnake might be back at the aircraft factory, so I can go there, but . . . thirty-six hours!

Down in the communal kitchen, Catnip and I share a meal of raw oats and vegetable broth with the pack rats next door. Catnip steamed some white rice and put out some dry rice so that everyone can nibble on those. A family of Shries who live on the floor below us come in with a breadstick and some more rice. Together we eat what we have shared in a friendly environment. Whether it be a nice fat roasted human thigh or this simple fare, the fellowship of shared dining is one of the key nutrients of eating. This is the natural way to live.

After gnawing on a rice kernel I sniff out my fellows to find Catnip, who holds a piece of the breadstick between her front paws, chewing on it as if she were a Dinosaur eating corn on the cob.

"Sister," I greet her. "I plan on being in Universal City for a while. And I need to find some of my friends from the colony."

"You're going to the service conference," she chirps excitedly. "That's great! I'm afraid I can't help you with your friends."

"They can squat in the back at the meetings," I add. "Then we can have the real meetings between the meetings."

Catnip's fur gets that glow about it, then she pops her eyes out of her skull in that classic ratty sign of contentment. "I'm sure glad you're getting back into mainstream life," she purrs.

"I'm just glad to have a home." I know what I'm saying. Home isn't just a roof to crawl into for a good day's sleep, but the community of fellows with whom we share our lives.

I take the bus to the Central Office to sniff for Cat Claw, or anyone else who I might know. I scurry through its halls and check out the huge conference room, but with no success. The conference center smells of the urine from practically every one of our species, and I smell Rodentia in our urine. It drives me back into service. Yet the fear of arrest hasn't left me, either.

I smell a pack rat, and I know him from somewhere. He's a he, I can tell by his aroma. "Excuse me, Brother Pack Rat," I address him. "I want to contact the office of Comrade Cat Claw."

Pack Rat sniffs me out with the suspicion we all share toward one another. "I know you, don't I?" he asks.

"How am I supposed to know who you know, brother?" I respond.

He backs up as his fur comes up on his back a little. Not completely hostile but heading that way.

I relax, tune into the inner power I learned in the white box, and I count to ten. "Brother, I want to go to the Service Conference in Universal City. And I need to make contact with some friends of mine before we go."

"Who's 'we'?" asks Pack Rat.

"Fellow trusted servants to the Union," I answer.

"That's not an answer!" squeals the pack rat.

"I was Comrade Cat Claw's superior until, maybe, I don't know, four months ago . . ."

"That's forever ago! You could have been a spy for Argentina! Maybe . . . you're one *now*!" The pack rat's bristles raise to the ceiling after this tirade.

I have no choice now but either to fight him, which would be a bad idea, or . . . be honest. "You're absolutely right, brother. Only . . . I was innocent."

"Nobody's innocent!" squeals the pack rat. "You're a spy!"

"Then so are you!" I squeal. I turn around to scamper away, but then the pack rat retreats first. I don't know what to do. The colony taught me to kill this rat if I needed to, but my intuition tells me something else. "Brother, that was wrong of me to accuse you of such a crime," I chirp with sincerity.

Pack Rat drops his angry dander, then stands up. "Brother, most of my family is in the colonies right now."

"And they haven't been released?" I chirp.

"No, and they won't be released if I don't watch every step I take!"

My soul grieves for this rat. I chirp out bitterly with sincere sorrow for my brother, the pack rat held hostage by our insanity. He sniffs me out in suspicion.

"Brother, I just returned from the colonies. I hope your family will return to you," I offer with the hope he will be comforted.

His disposition softens. He gnaws thoughtfully on the woodwork for a minute, then he turns to me. "Brother Fearless?"

"Yes, Brother Pack Rat," I answer.

"Come with me."

I follow him over a pile of human papers that will be chewed up into fire starter and nests for our siblings. We scurry into a storage space containing human boxes filled with our records. My pack rat brother crawls into a box, scratches through a stack of new records, sniffs them, and then puts them into his mouth. He crawls through a hole in the box to meet me.

"These are the latest arrivals from the colonies," he chirps. He offers the files to me, then as I take them, he adds, "But I need them back."

After a while, I have all the names and places I need. I write all the information down on a chunk of human paper ripped from the pile, then I roll it up. Before I put it in my mouth, I scurry up to him. He takes the sensitive information from me by biting onto it and pulling it out of my muzzle.

"Thank you, Brother Pack Rat," I share with him as he fusses with the files in his mouth. "I hope we can heal from this daymare we've been living through." He flicks his bushy wood rat tail in approval, then scampers away.


The list leads me to a tree in Cheeseman Park. There I smell the unmistakable nutty aroma of my chipmunk friend Soprano. We meet, but the little striped bushy-tailed troublemaker acts as though he doesn't know me.

One of his pups scampers up to me and cleans one of my ears.

"Woodchip," I greet her. At least she smells like the Woodchip from Soprano's litter.

"Get away from him!" Soprano whistles at his daughter.

"But I know this rat! He was always good to me," Woodchip responds.

"Don't matter! He's not one of us."

"Who are we, then?" Woodchip asks. I expect retribution against her. Soprano nips at her hinder parts, and she scampers away with a sad whimper. "Look what you're doing! You want to break us apart!" hisses the chipmunk.

I hit back with, "How long are you going to nurse this grudge against me?"

The chipmunk squirms, bites at imaginary fleas under his thigh, then he quiets himself. He cocks his head in my direction, and confesses, "Why didn't the Big Bunny ever come and talk to me?"

"I don't know," I answer.

"That's what broke my faith in Mother Rabbit. She'd send her only kit and kin into this world, but wouldn't come to her longsuffering servant, Soprano Cheekcheekchirblchickle! If, Shay 383, she has truly talked to you, why didn't you ask her to include me?"

That's what I figured. Soprano envies me for my experience. And he senses it really has happened. I'm at a loss. I mean, what do you squeak at envy?

The others all want to go with me. Blacksnake was in the main office of the aircraft factory, trying to get his old job back. And he's enrolled in morning school! He's bringing his school stuff with him.

Cappuccino was looking for me. We found each other at the hospital in the tunnel spaces under the liberated capitol building. We can hear the sounds and feel the vibrations of our RLA fighting in the tunnels against the Dinosaurs who have been holding out in that subterranean city under ours. And Spunky Kcherkcherktesherk, that bushy-tailed embodiment of communal wisdom and bearer of such a beautiful intellect, was trying to get back to his underground hovel in the northern Rockies. I met him right inside the Tivoli train station. He supported himself by stealing whatever food he could. He won't have to steal anymore. That is, if he doesn't want to. Such a way of living for us rodents. Stealing. So Rodentian. Yes, you can even say, ratty.

## Chapter Thirty

# VIRGINS TO THE CITY

Spunky and I enjoy the subtle vibrations of our maglev train, which dissipate as we enter into the station under the Five Burrows—the city the Dinosaurs named the Five Burroughs. The trip takes only about twenty-five minutes. Unlike our two-week trip from the Yukon to Denver on the plague train.

The maglev train comes to a stop.

"Attention! Attention! Your attention, please! Siblings, we have just arrived at Comrade Steely Terminal. Please gather your belongings and begin making your way to the open doors."

The doors open with a slam, and we exit. Another voice comes over the PA system on the train, "Squat clear of the closing doors, please!"

Cat Claw leads our group along. Both he and I have been here to Universal City, the de facto capital city of the world. I feel as though I've come back to a family who loves me a lot and wants me to succeed. And that family will do anything to challenge me, just to make me stronger. Oh, how good it is, to be back here.

We take an electric train to Universal City's Central Terminal, just under the government district of our capital. After getting settled in our temporary hovels by building nests and peeing on our personal spaces, we go to the General Service Office Executive Feeding Trough. Peektah meets us at the door dressed in an old, mousy-smelling field uniform.

"Well, smell what the cat drug all the way in from Denver!" squeaks the mouse. He scurries up to each of us, sniffing us out, and wiggling his long, mousy whiskers.

"Peektah!" whistles Spunky. "I though you got eaten by a cat."

"No, I stowed away on the first maglev train I could. And I got a new job working here at Central Office."

"Cheese tester?" asks Cappuccino.

"You and your damned anti-Mousian stereotypes!" Peektah squeals with hostility.

"I'm sorry," replies Cappuccino. "That sounded species-ist. I take it back with my sincerest regrets."

"All right. You're forgiven."

We go into the trough, to the feeders made from some Dinosaur's rain gutter. The gutter is clean and bare.

"When do they serve?" asks Cat Claw.

"Didn't you read the sign?" squeals a Dzumban in a pressed white uniform covered with a white dzash jacket.

"What sign?" replies Peektah the mouse.

"The sign out front!" the Dzumban waiter answers.

I scurry over to the entrance to sniff the space out, and I find the sign. "We regret to inform you, good siblings, this feeding establishment is temporarily closed until a fresh supply of food can be procured. We sincerely apologize for the inconvenience this imposes on you, our valued guests."

So shortages hit the very pinnacle of power as well! We're doomed if we can't feed ourselves.

Peektah stands up. "That's why I'm here, siblings. Follow me."

The mouse connects us with a cup of hot soup, dried breadcrumbs, and a nice oily slab of that delicious deep-fried pork skin found here in the Burrows, chicharrón.

As we enjoy our dinner, the mouse shares with us, "I've lived in this town for most of my life. I know how to survive here."

Cat Claw finishes his hunk of pork skin then addresses the mouse, "Brother mouse, please, be our guide here."

"Accepted," squeaks the mouse.


After our nourishment, we make our way to the Central Office Business Space, where service work to Rodentia languishes under the oppressive egos of the capstone. Nobody socializes here in the Business Space. Each delegation sits with its own species. But since we're observers we sit on the periphery. Cat Claw is a district committee member from the Rocky Mountain Front, so he can cast a vote if he wants to. As a former chairmouse, I expect I'll get some good attention on a muzzle-to-muzzle basis, but the coordinators of the Business Space, what we call CenBusSpa, aren't going to invite me up to lead the meetings.

At the end of the night, the acting chairlady, a chipmunk from eastern Canada takes the stand.

"Thank you for coming out here tonight. It's been a very productive business gathering, and I think we're on the road to recovery from our sad loss several weeks ago. As we all know, no one rodent represents Rodentia, any more than any one species does. Before we close tonight, I'd like to entertain the audience. For any of our observers who would like to share, we have a microphone set up at each side of the assembly hall here. I'm sure you've heard the delegates squeaking from those microphone stations. So . . . if any of you would?" After that, the chipmunk sits down, and I pop up, scampering to the microphone.

"Is this thing on?" I ask, like such an amateur. "I am Fearless Litzkachew, one-time chairmouse of the Ninth All Rodents International." You can hear a bug break his wind right now.

"Chairmouse Fearless," comes a voice from the audience. Familiar, but I don't know whose.

"As I said, I am a former chairmouse and a fellow friend to all of you in service. I was released from one of the colonies . . ."

"Which colony?" comes a squeak from what sounds like a mouse.

". . . The ROCOCOLACO colony," I answer. "So I'm back, and I want to share an observation with you all. If there's ever a legacy we can pass on to our future generations, it's the legacy of *unity*. From many, one! This governing body needs to get grounded on that most essential element."

"Excuse me, Comrade Fearless," the chairlady chipmunk interjects. "This service body is only commissioned to give trusted service. It does not govern."

"Thank you, Comrade Chairlady. Anyway, I would like to

bring something back to this assembly at the summer solstice. What I want to do is provide an agenda of change with our direction as a service body."

"And what needs to change?" comes a voice from the main group of Dzumbani.

"I'm not going to get into specifics right now. I want to come as a fully prepared trusted servant. And I don't have a position in service right now."

"Time, Comrade Fearless," the sergeant of arms at the door whistles.

"Thank you," I chirp into the microphone, then give the mic to the marmot looming over me, waiting to whistle to the assembly.

After the meeting, I gather with Peektah, Cat Claw, Spunky, and Cappuccino. We meet over a saucer of tea, brewed then poured into the dish with no frills or honey. I don't care. The tea is pretty good. Nearby, the teapot, an old tin can with a spout bent into one side, steams on two bricks over a fire.

I lap up the hot tea. "Did I make any sense in there?"

"Why would you ask such an insecure question," Spunky responds, then laps up some tea from his side of the saucer.

"I don't know. I do have my work cut out for me. That I know," comes my answer. "But about that agenda, I don't know what I'm going to pull together."

Cat Claw slurps up some tea, then he hits me with, "Don't do it alone! We all stand together in this. And you rodents need a project to occupy yourselves with. Whatever it is you want to do, you ought to start working it up, and working these rooms to make it happen."

"I want to end our senseless war against the co-ops, for one. Then I want to restructure how we fight the just war we're in," I state in between lapping up tea.

"And what just war are we in?" asks Peektah.

I take a breath, and look him in his beady eyes, "The sacred war against humanity!" I squeal.

"Do you know," Cappuccino asks me, "It's been over one hundred nights since the war started?"

"What does that have to do with anything now, Cappuccino? I knew before this war started that all the cat scat about killing the last cat and the other human before a live audience for the whole animal kingdom to enjoy was just a lot of unfounded optimism. I always knew a victorious war to free the Earth from human blight would have to be a multigenerational, evolutionary process. We have to be in it for the long haul. And . . . we can't be fighting *each other*!"

Cat Claw steps in, "How are you going to convince this ingrown body of pompous rodents to change? You only have a past. Not a present within this service structure."

I'm stumped. And I hate the pressure that this former underling puts on me now that he's established, and I'm trying to get my paws on solid ground. "Well," I conclude. "We'll figure it out."

"Use your support base here," Cat Claw offers, pointing his muzzle at our companions around the tea saucer. But I'm thinking of something a lot bigger.

## Chapter Thirty-One

# I WANT TO SERVE

The maglev got us back to Denver in less than an hour. So getting between these two powerful metropolitan centers is easy. But we have virtually no contact with the body politic of our Union, the foundation of the pyramid. Getting to the new capstone in Universal City was easy. But I want to go throughout the body of the Union.

The All Rodents Evolutionary Union is shaped like a pyramid. The leadership is at the top—what I call the capstone. Under it, the main body of the Union consists of the many strata of social stations, which I refer to collectively as the membership. The main body should always be united with the capstone. Never should a gap separate the two. Under Steely, a gulf grew between us.

My task, as Fearless Litzkachew, Shriedaygahbah with a pointy Shrie muzzle and a long black tail, is to bridge that gap. If I can do that, maybe we, as a species, can bridge the other gaps separating us. And another thing . . . above everything, I am an animal, I got to add. I feel good about being one.

I go immediately to our Central Service Office in Denver.

"I am here to serve," I proclaim to a gopher behind a front desk.

Stunned silence comes from the Gopherian receptionist and the half dozen bureaucratic types behind her. They freeze with their muzzles pointed at me, then all pour out a peepy wave of laughter.

"And what's so funny about that?" I demand.

"I'm sorry," the gopher whistles, as she sniffs me out, "But who are you?"

"I am . . ." I cut myself off midsentence, feeling something in my subconscious about my whole approach. "I'm sorry. I'm being presumptuous. I do apologize."

The group of rodents goes into peepy hysterics all over again.

"Would you please leave? Or I'm going to call security on you," the gopher states. I slink out of the Service Office like a garter snake. Now, how am I going to serve?

I scurry along a ditch. Water flows by, and I think about that sluice box in the colony. Soprano told me water holds spirits, life energy that creates its own personality. Perhaps one will ride up out of the water and direct my attention. I hear the buzz of a chainsaw over my head. I look up to see a flying something circling me. Is it a wasp? Is it a hawk? It drops down, and its two-stroke motor oil smell tells me it's one of our aircraft. The flying object lands, then taxis right up to me. The motor kicks off.

"Is that Fearless?" I hear from the cockpit in a voice I haven't heard in *months*. I bristle up, just a little.

"Morgana! What are you doing in this town?" I reply.

"Wait a minute!" squeals my half-sister Morgana Fairy Foot from the pilot's side of her personal aircraft. And no, Daddy didn't buy it for her. And yes, I don't care if she's family. We're related but we don't relate.

She slithers out of the cockpit onto the concrete and scurries up to me. We sniff each other out, like happy family members do, but I still keep my guard up.

"Fearless, don't you recognize your sister after all these months?"

"Of course, Sister Fay," I answer. My resonance stands guarded, to squeak the least.

"I've looked all over the whole continent for you. I hope you don't reject me now."

"Well, Sister Morgana, I never hated you or anything, but . . ."

"You're still a divinity hater, aren't you?" Morgana hasn't been able to keep up with me.

"As a matter of fact, I have a practice I enjoy," I respond.

"That's great!" she replies. "I hope you experience joy with it. I do my rituals at least once a week. My weeks come in nine-night sequences. One for every number in the Pythagorean theorem."

She shares about some Dinosaur who developed some math magic. I, myself, am a language- and history-oriented type. "I have to make it back to Universal City," I add, almost wishing I hadn't. Sis always had a pull on my spirit ever since we were young.

"Let me help you," she adds.

I feel her qi pull on me, and I know of only one way to break it. "Please, let me handle my life alone!"

"Bad mistake! You've never outgrown this, have you?" she responds.

"I'm just not connected to you, that's all."

She leaps at me. I dodge her, but then gather up my qi to fight her.

"Don't ever insult me like that again, ever!" she shrieks. Her qi wounds my soul with its power, and I feel my spirit break from her attack. I pull away from her, though animal aggression must be met with something greater. But I don't have it. "Don't scamper away!" she adds.

"Morgana! You're not in my life anymore!" She backs up at my rejection. "I don't want to interact with you until your energy changes."

She scampers to her plane, and I head back to the roof I share with Catnip.

"I don't know whether to love you or hate you at this point!" she shrieks at me. Will those be her parting words to me? Oh, to be so fortunate.

The salon gathers itself together around a plastic lid of sorts, filled with apple cider from some Dinosaur's stash. We lap up the cider and lay out our plan to retake our Union. To the best of my ability, I bounce back from the confrontation with my sister. But I don't regret it came. I still feel drained in my soul, though. As the dirty Dinosaurs would put it, "You can pick your friends, and you can pick your muzzle, but you can't pick you relatives."

Spunky holds the piece of register paper in his paws as he announces, "Alright, everybody. Here are the new items we would like to see the Union take on for itself now that War Collectivism has done enough damage to us."

I listen, but I am not here in my soul. Yet I want to be. The stuff we're coming up with is just what I can believe in.

Spunky hands the piece of paper to Cappuccino, who wiggles her whiskers on her blunt, Dzumban muzzle. "Parts of the platform for ratification by the general assembly of the Tenth All Rodents International:

Number One. Communal, not collective. We will become a Union of communities, self-supporting in their conduct, autonomous and sovereign in their direction.

Number Two. We will make peace with the Co-Op Leagues, starting with an immediate cease-fire. We will follow with a commitment to building goodwill with all rodent groups and societies and civilizations, whether they join the Union or not.

Number Three. We will sell off all the means of production to the various housing, gardening, and industrial co-operatives that will be formed by the workers, gardeners, and dwellers who will invest in those co-operatives.

Number Four. Private as well as public enterprise will be encouraged.

"And championed," I add. Cappuccino continues.

Number Five. We will refuse to take a loan from anyone, or any entity! Instead, we will create a currency backed by a monetary reserve including precious and non-precious metals, hemp, and its female companion, what we know in Standard Ratsqueak as Erb.

Number Six. Every lishek, co-op, or other single unit of social grouping will be fully autonomous, except in matters affecting the others, or the All Rodents Evolutionary Union as a whole.

Number Seven. Every lishek, community, co-op, etcetera, shall be fully self-supporting, never depending on others unless under attack from the Humans.

Number Eight. The All Rodents Evolutionary Union will be exclusive of religions. Everyone will be free to celebrate their own faith or non-faith. And no cult of personality, or any other kind, will be permitted to vex the souls of our fellow rodents."

Cappuccino sits down, and we all take it in. "How much of this will be accepted?" asks Blacksnake.

I step in. "We may never see any of this come to pass. But what I'm thinking is we go throughout the areas we hold. We go in, brag up what we're doing. We communicate directly with our siblings."

Cat Claw, who has remained silent through most of the conference, steps up. "I might be able to get you a train to take you everywhere you need to go."

"Maybe we can go to specific places and spread out," offers Cappuccino.

I point my muzzle at Cat Claw. "Would we be able to go in a week?" I ask.

"At the latest. Let's just go with what we have. The message we have will be powerful enough to carry itself," he answers.

"Then it's a week from now?" I ask.

"We'll make it a week from now. Plan an itinerary beforehand, and we will see where we can get to."

## Chapter Thirty-Two

# BONDS OF HEALING

As the evening breaks over the roof where my catnippy Catnip and I live, she sniffs my ratty thorn, then gives it a warm, tonguey lick. "Delish," she purrs.

She lifts up her tail for me. I sniff her butthole, then worship her lady rat parts, praying a prayer of gratitude with my tongue to Nature for her creation.

"Shee! Get away from me!" shrieks my partner, bounding away from me as if I were a blazing flame. I don't know what to do.

"Catnip . . . I am beyond words," I chirp with sorrow.

"Please, bite me! Rip me to thorning pieces!" This hysteria of hers rips my soul apart. This isn't her. Then she chirps bitterly.

She's the girl rat I love. And we never just "thorned." We always made love, just as we were this evening. But now I see her when we were both arrested, and that violence against our souls and bodies wasn't just against each of us, but against the union of our spirits and souls. Now the violation burns my soul.

"Let's go get some chocolate," I recommend.

"Why?" she weeps.

"Something to take the pain away," I answer.

"No," she chokes out, "I want to be strong through this. I don't want to anesthetize."

Then I sense another force among us. A loving presence observes the two of us. "Let Nature and her god be your strength, and your joy," I blurt out, not knowing what I squeak. Then both of us fall silent.

We spend the rest of our evening in that silence, broken only by her occasional peepy weeping. Those mournful chirps torture me more than anything the RexCom traitors did to me. I want to touch her, bathe her with my love, and know my affection will wash away all that trauma. I don't know how to bring it up to her. So I leap in.

"Catnip . . . Sister. I don't know how to help you, but I want to. What do you need right now?"

"Don't leave me!" she squeals. But in five nights, I go on a public relations campaign to awaken the soul of our Union.

I sniff her ear. She bites me, and I wince, but then she chirps bitterly.

"Catnip," I gently peep. "I want you to go on a campaign with me."

"Why?" she hisses.

"So you'll always be with me," I answer.

"Thorn your Nature-damned service work!" she shrieks. I back away. "Don't wince!" she bitterly squeals. I'm so pulled back and forth from all of this that I jump over her in angst. I land, then spin around to go muzzle-to-muzzle with her.

"Catnip!" I squeak with authority, taking control of the situation. "You need to meditate!"

"What?"

"Yes, meditate!" I take a ratty meditation pose with my front paws dangling in front of me. "Like this!"

She mirrors my stance. "Yes?"

"Now, for the next five minutes . . ."

"We don't have any timepiece."

"We'll *guestimate* it," I state. "Now, breathe in slowly, through you nose . . ." We do this in unison. ". . . Then breathe out through your muzzle." We do this for a moment, then I add the other aspect of this breath exercise. "Now imagine a pretty white light of love and healing coming through that tiny spot between your eyes, right at the bridge of your nose . . . Let it flow in there, and travel down the front of your body . . . then let it settle in the bottom of your belly where your womb takes her place. With each breath, I want you to imagine your womb filling up with that beautiful love and healing. Just imagine your girl rattiness being cleansed with each breath, every white light breathed into your womb."

"And the exhale?" she asks.

"Okay," I answer. "After you hold the breath and the white light for a second . . ."

"That's a long time to hold your breath!" she squeals.

"Well, work with it. You'll want to find your natural rhythm. You'll get a strong sense of what your body wants. What you'll do—what we'll do—is to breathe that white light right out of your sacrum across your spine, till you see in your mind's eye the white light pour out the top of your head."

We practice all of this for a few minutes. I don't know how she's doing with it, but I sense in the connection we have, that she's calming down. At least her mind doesn't chew on that ugly wound to her soul for the time being.

"I have to go," she purrs. Then she gives me an affectionate sniffing. I lick her fur, and I feel her soul. She has hope in her aura. That's more delicious to me than her girly parts.

Chapter Thirty-Three

# WHISTLE-STOP

The steam train pulls out of our subterranean station. I love the cloud of steam that smells of burning coal. We, the fearless Agitprop Committee as I like to think of us, venture out into Rodentia's heart and soul! We project ourselves on the iron millipede out of the comfort of the earth, into the vulnerability of the open space that is Nebraska, our first destination.

Catnip bounces up to me. "You have the most delicious aura! Mmm, I can taste it!" We sniff each other out, oh, so affectionately. I feel her soul healing already. All her trauma will melt away as its ugly power gives way to the beauty of post-traumatic growth.

Our itinerary includes the great prairie land to the east, then down to the coast of the Great Ocean of the Setting Sun. It will be a few weeks, but I sense what we are doing will touch our species like nothing else.

Night falls. In the comfort car, we spread out our ideas and argue, dream, and enjoy the hope of a new future. Before us, the destiny of our superorganism lies.

Back in Denver, Comrade Blacksnake scurries to a platform in front of a large group of rodents gathered in what was once a warehouse.

"Comrades! Siblings! Thank you for showing up to hear what needs to be squeaked! Over the last eight months, we gave up our power to a false hope. I want to see us reclaim our power! You, brother! Sister! You are the bearers of our power . . ." Blacksnake waits for the response, which never comes. "We have a former trusted servant . . . I met him when we were in the colony . . ."

"Which one?" squeals a house mouse in a clean, green dzash.

"I don't know which one. It was way up north of here. But his name is Fearless Litzkachew. He wants to go to Universal City and clean up our Union from the top down. But he's just one rat. All of us together have a job to do . . ."

"We're too busy trying to survive as it is!" an emaciated Dzumban pouts.

"You're wasting your energy on surviving!" responds Blacksnake. "I don't want to rip down your situation, but this Union has a destiny to fulfill! You play a role in it! Tell Universal City you want Fearless as your next general secretary!"

Cappuccino flies aboard a twin engine transport to a makeshift airstrip on a stretch of interstate not far from Lake Michigan. She bounces around with some cardboard boxes in the middle and some RLA officials between those and the cockpit.

"Hold on, everyone!" comes a shriek over the intercom. "We're taking evasive action!"

The interior shifts, throwing Cappuccino into weightlessness. She swirls her tail and tries to grab whatever she can with her jaws. The floor of the cabin comes up to her, knocking the wind out of her. Then she's weightless again, until the side of the fuselage slams her. She grabs some part of the interior, she doesn't know which, and fastens her incisors to it.

Outside, a flying machine approaches her plane. Under its gray fuselage, the aircraft's metal and glass eye looks her way, and focuses on her plane. Then a 7.62mm six-barreled Gatling gun awakens from its lethargy, points at her plane, and waits to burp hot death into Cappuccino while she hangs on the side of the fuselage.

The antagonist feels the steel talons of the warbird in charge of escorting my dear friend Cappuccino. The propeller of the pilotless enemy seizes up in black smoke, and crankcase oil rains a black rain horizontally from the burning motor. Gravity pulls Cappuccino in a spin, then everything balances out. Cappuccino loses her grip on the bulkhead of the fuselage, drops down to the floor, and sniffs for her assigned seat.

"Stay in your seats, everybody. Where's there's one drone, there are several others!" comes the voice over the intercom. Cappuccino fastens herself into the floor of the plane and loves the Earth like she never has before.

Peektah approaches a group of rodents at the General Service Office under the Great Hall of Evolution. He feels sharp as cheddar in his freshly pressed light blue dzash, showing his union affiliation as a district committee leader. Before he went to the colony, other rodents, mostly rats, bullied him about. But now, he goes forth on all fours, proud of his survival skills. This town swallowed him up like a garter snake, but he's back, and he's going to be the boa constrictor!

"Fellahs," he squeaks to the group. "A delegation of Rodentia's brightest minds will be here for the Tenth International and I want them to enjoy a big, Five Burrows welcome from this service office. Would you all be so kind as to join me at a pre-conference meeting later this night? Precisely at pre-dawn?"

"Piss off, mousy!" whistles a gray squirrel. The other extend the courtesy of ignoring him.

Peektah finishes the short conversation with "As you wish."

Back home in the northern Rockies, not far from what the humans still call Lake Louise, Spunky squats before his fellow co-op members at a Co-operative League conference held in an abandoned barn on the grounds of a logging camp.

"To all my friends and fellows in this co-operative, I want to say how good it is to be free from the terrible bondage I was in just north of here. We're surrounded by camps and colonies the All Rodents Evolutionary Union built for rodents like us. Anyone who is sovereign in their souls. But in those camps and colonies, I met rodents who weren't brainwashed by the insanity created in Universal City. I met our fellows in there, as well as former and current members of the Union, rodents with a vision. Fellow rodents who want peace with us. There's a group of our animal siblings who right now work to establish peace with us. I will whistle to you today that we have a hope of peace with the All Rodents Evolutionary Union."

"Preach that hope when you smell your burrow burning after it's been hit by the RLA!" whistles a gopher. The ground squirrel hears nothing. Maybe because of suspicion.

A porcupine stands up in the audience and answers the attack. "Brother, we can't trust the Union, but we can use peace to prepare ourselves to fight them."

"What do you know about defense?" the gopher angrily whistles.

"I carry my personal defense with me, everywhere!" the porcupine answers, inviting a round of laughter from the whole crowd.

"It's not funny!" cries the gopher. "I lost my first family to an air assault attack. They fell out of the sky on their cheebahs. All of them! Rats."

"Brother!" hisses Spunky. "The rodents in the Union are dying in slave labor colonies just north of here. We need to make peace with those who want peace!"

"Why?" demands the gopher.

"Because the humans have been doing it to us, too," answers Spunky. "And they want to destroy this planet. They're even building a death star! It's in one of their movies."

The gopher throws at Spunky, "What if we end up fighting the humans?"

Spunky responds, "Then we'll have to cooperate, won't we?"

Our train arrives at an improvised stop, the same as it has over the last two weeks, where members of our Union come out to hear our team present to them a song, a dance, and a speech by me. No one else among our team on this train likes to squeak publicly. I love it. I like an audience! And I love to get up in front of a crowd and work the room.

I scurry out into the night air, breathe it in with a strong joy of life, and take my place in front of a group of about six hundred warriors and local militia fighters of both genders dressed in their blue field uniforms. Gathered with them, pups and rodents dressed in work clothes, or nothing at all, take their place in a horseshoe-shaped gathering in front of an old dresser drawer with a microphone on it, connected to a liberated radio adapted to be a PA system and karaoke machine. I take my place on that dresser drawer.

"Siblings, I smell the delicious aroma of canvas web gear and rifle oil. I enjoyed my time in service to our species as a front commander in the Rockies. And I always enjoy being with you, my fellow fighters for the All Rodents Evolutionary Union. Our species and our Union have been through a time of trial, and I hope we can come out of it alive. I believe we can.

"I think while I've been, I don't know how to put it, but . . ." I really am without words to talk. I want us all to have a connection, a bond, so that I can awaken that power that is within us as a species. ". . . I smell within us a power. And it's a power of nature . . ."

"Just spit it out, tail hole! We don't have all month!" chirps a field mouse.

"Shee, don't waist our time, you kitty thorner," a kangaroo rat peeps in that indescribable accent their species has when squeaking in Standard Ratsqueak. I'm losing my audience. Tough crowd, tonight.

A house mouse wearing his helmet with helmet netting on it stands up and squeals, "Cat! I can smell it! Over there!"

I sniff the air around us and sure enough! That blurry thing right behind me crouches! I can tell it's a feral cat, furry, and black! It's moving! I ain't squatting down for a thorned-in-the-butthole cat! "Come on, Kitty!" I shriek as my fur bristles up. The black beast pounces, and I jump at its soft underbelly. I bite Kitty hard with our great natural weapon, my incisors, rodent incisors, and part of its guts explodes in my jaws. This miniature black panther easily swings his paw over, batting me in my ratty muzzle. I don't feel the scratch, but I know it's there. He's flexible, more than I am. And faster, in all his martial moves. But I'm not going to cower before a cat!

"Bring a pee sac kicker!" I squeal, in reference to the portable antihuman rocket launcher made from recycled plastic, about the size of a cigarette. I hear the report of the rocket, then the cat jerks with me on its back. I continue to bite the thorner, then get him between his shoulder blades. He lets out a hideous hiss, then slaps me with a free paw. My face gets ripped, but I don't let loose.

He tries crawling away from the group, but he can only use his front legs. He bites at me with his massive black jaws, and I feel his fangs in me. But I bite him again, right above his heart, and he goes limp and loose. I jump away from him. He points his fangy face at me and hisses again, but his hiss loses its enthusiasm. Then he folds his head into his front paws. I approach, as other siblings join me. Then the cat springs up and slaps at me again.

We all bounce back. A Dzumban in that green camouflage combat uniform approaches me with a pee sac kicker in his jaws. I take it, shoulder it, and aim behind the black cat's pointy ears. The third gender of humanity looks at me, then rubs its head vigorously, yet the cat's energy dwindles. It growls in that soprano-pitched growl, as if to say, "Go ahead! Kill me! I regret nothing!" I squeeze the firing mechanism, and the projectile reaches out to the cat's medulla oblongata, and it takes care of the rest. I drop the empty, hot plastic tube, and feel sorry for this four-legged human. There is such a nobility about this adversary. That's what I sense. Feral, yet honorable.

"Fearless got ripped up," someone whispers behind me. "He's still squatting, and that cat's nature-damned dead."

"That's one tough mother thorner," a burly Dzumban whispers.

## Chapter Thirty-Four

# TENTH INTERNATIONAL

The warmth of spring fills our nights with hope, as does the delicious aroma of clover growing around our apartment complex. Catnip busies herself with last-minute tasks before we depart for Universal City. The Tenth All Rodents International Convention convenes over the last four nights of spring, ending with elections for the top service positions of the General Service Administration. Yes, GenServAd. Or as we put it in Standard Ratsqueak, *Dzeesh-BeechDah*.

I go in the capacity of the newly elected alternate general service officer of the Cheeseman Park Co-Operative. Cat Claw was the GSO until he resigned to take a position at Regional, and we still don't have a replacement for him. I'm stuck with all the work anyway, but what the humanity? At least I get to eat tonight. And breathe fresh mountain air. And drink good water!

Later, after settling into our nests on the maglev train, I stretch my muzzle over to my delicious-smelling lady rat. Catnip winces from my attention, and my whiskers tickle her fur, to get a sense of what's wrong.

"Sorry," she apologizes. "That struck me as . . . weird."

"There's nothing weird about loving my woman," I squeak with authority.

Catnip relaxes. "Fearless, give me a break. I really love you. Just don't . . ." She cuts off her apology with sad peepy weeping.

"I'm here for you," I chirp. I refuse to be a fair-weather lover for my special someone.

She moves away from me. Her nest gets farther from me as the nights roll on. And I feel like human scat on the sidewalk because of it.

With the twenty-four-minute trip to the Eastern Coast underway, I occupy myself with what has become the great recreation and pastime of my life. I quiet myself, breathe in several breaths, and tune up my chakras. I'm working on the ones on my paws, and that earth one, but in this electromagnetically floating millipede, I don't know how grounded to the Earth I can be. We stop a few times, but I take it all in in a scurry. Then I remain silent, thinking only on an imaginary irrigation ditch, babbling along under a full moon.

"We will be arriving at Grand Central Terminal in approximately six minutes. Please gather all your belongings and leave nothing behind for us to throw out. Thank you for riding MagnetoGo!" The conductor finishes the announcement, while I pull myself back to the foundational reality that is my physical life. Yet I feel Catnip pulling on my soul's power through the bonds we share, though she doesn't want to get close to me.

I grab all my stuff, three bags total. I sniff out Catnip, who brought nine bags. I'm so glad she left all her other stuff at home. I don't care if the chipmunks get into it. She drops one of the pouches, then keeps scouring, unaware of her loss.

"Catnip!" I whistle. She jumps at my call. "Wait!"

"We need to get off this train!" she chirps back at me.

"You dropped a pouch," I answer. I pick it up in my jaws, and scurry up to her, putting the lost pouch in her muzzle. She wiggles her whiskers over it, then takes it, tying it together with the other eight. I check mine. All present and accounted for.

"Thanks," she chirps with a softer, more inviting spirit. We make our way to the next train that will take us to the General Service District of Universal City, where the Great Hall of Evolution stands. On the way to our destination, we rock back and forth to the clack-clack of the electric train going over rails freshly laid by slave labor. Catnip leans over to me, her whiskers tickling my ear. "I love you, Fearless, I really do," she peeps.

"Lean into me," I instruct. She obeys, squeezing her body up against mine. "Now, feel the joy of being with your rat." She sniffs me out, and I feel her body relax. Our stop waits two stations ahead of us. I pour a white light of love and healing out across my soul to hers, blanketing her body with that beautiful power. We can't even see the color gold, but it don't matter. I'm here for her, and I think she's good with that.


Catnip embodies our beloved Union, as does our Dzumban friend Cappuccino. I made it my life's work to submit myself these many, short months of my life to her welfare. Both these girls bear the scars in their souls of the brutality of Nature's dark side; the negative side of life, where the hunger for power can never be satisfied.

I scurry to the Great Hall of Evolution under a beautiful late spring sky. Above me, fluffy clouds are illuminated at their edges by the moon's glory. Oh, holy moon, how majestic you are in the deep blue heavens! I hear the sound of jets overhead as I approach the front door. The rumble of their airstrikes drifts like a current of ill wind to my ears. I sniff in that direction.

"You know, comrade, those Dinosaurs kill a hundred of their own kind every time they attack us," quips a Dzumban dressed in a starched green uniform. "They'll bomb themselves into extinction if we let them."

The fragrance of an untold number of flowers cocoons me as I scurry down the corridor. That flowery security blanket comforts me as I enter the auditorium. I take my place at the table for the delegates from the Rocky Mountain region. Our distinguished leader, Comrade Supreme Regional Service Representative Cat Claw, my onetime aide-de-camp, now my alpha in-service, sniffs me out, tickling me with his whiskers. "We just wrapped it up at the nominations committee, Comrade Fearless."

"You sound chirpy over all this," I mention.

"We have a fine list of candidates this assembly. Pay attention, Brother Fearless. You might be surprised who gets the nod."

He's thorning my head, again. Anyway, I still respect his service to us. The general assembly goes on. Tedious torture to the masses, that's what public service is. So as a result, the majority abrogates their rightful place as the leaders by delegating their leadership to the few, the proud political wonks who lap assemblies like this up like warm broth out of a spoon. Of course, for me, this is a banquet of its own. Yeah, I got to admit, I roll around in my wonkitude like a porky pig in hot mud. Okay, so I'm lovin' it! Sue me!

"The candidate from the Rocky Mountain Front, Comrade Fearless Litzkachew, Chairmouse of the Ninth All Rodents International, former commander of the Rocky Mountain Front and the Wabash Front . . ."

"Me?" I shriek. That rubs Cat Claw's fur wrong.

"Comrade, I'd rather see you in the GenSec position than take a chance on someone else. Like last time."

The blood flows out of my head. What if . . . oh, no. They won't vote me in, I assure myself. I'm a soul criminal. An enemy of the species.

The chairmouse calls my name over the PA system. This is my time to give an answer for myself. "Comrade," our chairmouse who happens to be a fat beaver from the Yukon somewhere near my one-time sweet little corner of hell says, "Will you squat for nomination for the service position of general secretary of the supreme secretariat of the General Service Office of the All Rodents Evolutionary Union?"

The luna moth lands on my shoulder. "Say 'Yes, I squat for the position,'" she whispers in my big Shrie ear. "And remember: In all storytelling, refusal of the call leads to sorrow later in the story."

"Wait a minute! Luna moths don't squeak!" That's what I shriek in my most excited, what-the-thorn disbelief.

Cat Claw interjects, "Just say 'Yes.'"

"Shut up!" I chirp bitterly at him.

"Comrade Fearless Litzkachew? Do I hear a yes or a no?" The voice from the chairbeaver resonates with authority.

"Would you please do it for us?" come two familiar voices, and I see clearly through my myopia both Cappuccino and Catnip squatting together, dressed in their medical corps uniforms. Like they just took a minute out of combat against humanity to give me their two cents' worth. My body relaxes, and I intuitively know what to do.

"Siblings, the Candidate Fearless Litzkachew squats! Yes!" I found my agreement to be most natural.

"Thank you," whistles the chairmouse who's really the chairbeaver.


The lists get read. Flyers become available with all our pertinent service history. They're pinned up on the different corkboards around the main hall and around the building. The burden of responsibility for leadership within this Union isn't watered down by distributing it all the way down to the vote of the individual citizen. If rodents want to serve our Union, let them show up at those gatherings we affectionately name lishek-conscience meetings, where the conscience of the fully autonomous and self-supporting individual lisheks direct the leadership. That is the foundation of service within our Union.

The chairmouse who's really a chairbeaver beats his wet flat tail by the microphone to call the election session assembly to order. We squat in our places.

"Siblings, comrades, welcome to tonight's session. I am Comrade Chairmouse Woody Mapleleaf, and I proudly serve the All Rodents Evolutionary Union."

The assembly, all one thousand of us, squeaks in unison, "Greetings, Comrade Mapleleaf!"

The Beaverian brother stands on his hind legs wrapping his webbed front paws around the microphone stand. He adjusts his starched light green dzash with brass wood shavings on the collar, denoting his authority among beavers. "The votes have been cast and counted . . ." I have a hard time getting through the beaver's whistled Beaverian accent, but he probably hates my big Shrie ears for some weird reason. ". . . And now the moment has arrived! We will have our distinguished Comrade Executive Service Officer to the Supreme Secretariat Spike Pincushion tally the votes as read."

Behind him the same porcupine who tallied the votes putting Steely in office waves his chalk stick in the air. Good to see he didn't get swept away in the Steelyist terror.

A Shrie sister joins the beaver at the podium. The beaver sniffs her, then whistles into the microphone, "Allow me to introduce this fine young sibling. Or would you like the honors?"

She takes the stand and puts her muzzle to the microphone. "I am Senior Fighter Shee K'rshreecheek, and I serve the All Rodents Evolutionary Union!"

"Greetings, Comrade Shee!" we all shriek as one.

She continues with her introduction. "I am happy to be of service to you all this evening. Please overlook the scar on my face. I got it killing a cat on the Malibu Front." A California Girl rat!

A house mouse struts up to the beaver with an envelope in his muzzle. The beaver sniffs the envelope and opens it up. After sniffing and nibbling on the sheet of paw-pressed paper inside, he pulls it out, unfolds it, and begins to read.

"I shall pass this to our brave fighter and official tallyer," whistles the beaver.

"That's 'tallyress'" she corrects. Nature, I hope we don't turn into the Humans! "Our official tally . . ."

"Excuse me! Excuse me!" opines the porcupine. "Aren't I the official vote tallyer and she's the announcetress?"

"Brother," the beaver answers. "Let's just go with it."

Sibling Shee the feisty Shrie reads from the sheet. "First, I want to thank the assembly for this honor of serving the Union. I'd like to do it in memory of my dear Shrie sister Senior Fighter Palmer Firewalker, who died fearlessly on the Spokane Front." My question is, who killed her? Silence fills the assembly, a moment of honor for the fallen firewalker. She then continues, "We had a total of nine hundred ninety-nine voting members. Our final count was one thousand three votes. We found forty-nine duplicates, plus four ineligible votes. So our final results come from the nine hundred fifty votes that will determine your choice for the next general secretary of the Supreme Secretariat. We had no abstentions. Thirty-two candidates gathered one third of the nine hundred fifty. Three hundred sixteen votes for thirty-two."

I break the block of wood I'm gnawing on with a disturbing crack. "Please forgive me," I whisper, feeling ill.

The sister continues, "Out of six hundred thirty-four votes for the five major candidates, we have the following results. Forty-three votes went to Comrade Spiffy Dzerrshketet of the Greater Los Angeles Front."

The assembly cheers the results in honor of the Dzumban brother.

"Forty-six votes went to Comrade Pork Ng'Chebeet who fights in the San Joachim Delta Front," Shee announces to a consolation applause for the lesser bandicoot from Stockton.

"Comrade Regional Service Representative Ulgharr 'Nutsy' Nutsohn, the tufted squirrel from Bemidji . . ."

"That's in the Western Scandahoovian Peninsula," Nutsy informs everyone at his table.

". . . Garnered eighty votes," Shee reads followed by an impassioned crescendo of applause for the stoic squirrel.

"Scurrying onward, our runner-up can be proud to receive eighty-two votes. Comrade Foxy Bushytail!" A stronger response than was received for the others fills the assembly hall as Sister Foxy, that fox squirrel bigger than a house cat, swishes her tail as she enjoys the consolation. The mood in the hall resonates like electricity in a lightning bolt. "Which leaves us with our next general secretary of the Supreme Secretariat. With three hundred eighty-three votes . . ."

"Shay 383!" I blurt out of my soul, feeling the horror our taxonomic order experienced.

". . . The chairmouse of the last All Rodents International . . ." she squeaks, and I poop, not knowing why I wretch at this experience. ". . . Comrade Fearless Litzkachew, all the way from liberated Denver!" The assembly explodes in a thunderous squeak! By popular demand of the capstone's new governing soul, I grasp that I am the new general secretary. I want to pass out.

Cappuccino and Catnip scamper up to me, both grabbing me for themselves. All three of us cuddle, love, and pee on one another. Every emotion an animal can experience pulses through my being. My physical body aches with the emotional overload. My etheric body shines through my physical conscience, shimmering warm and oh, so bright. I see, smell, and feel my whole soul stretching out from my body almost three inches from my core in my sacrum, even pointing out from my tail. I wiggle my whiskers at Shee the Shrie.

The chairmouse that's really a beaver takes the microphone. "We will have the acceptance speech from Comrade Fearless in ten minutes. In the event he declines, we will invite Comrade Foxy to become the next GenSec."

An eternity of ten whole minutes drags me to the podium, escorted by my significant other Catnip, and my faithful comrade in arms Cappuccino. I pass Foxy on the way. She flicks her tail in approval. Then she opens a peanut with her incisors.

At the podium, all my qi drains out of my body. Gingerly, I take my place at the mic. "At this point, all I can squeak is thank you, all of you who came to serve our Union and our order." A fresh power flows through my soul like a delicious, quenching drink of fresh water from a stream. "Yeah, I don't have anything else to say." I squawk as I move from the mic, then get up to it again. "Okay, let me add, thanks to all of you who voted for me, and all of you who voted for someone else!" Dead silence from over a thousand rodents. "This isn't a coronation. I'm making sure the inauguration won't be that. Our supreme secretariat isn't a rat king," I offer to the assembly. "I am not your future leader. I won't forget that we are not leaders, but trusted servants to our Union, and to each other. I am not your leader. I am your servant." I stop and think about that. "But that doesn't mean I'm your field mouse, either!" The silence shatters at the laughter from the assembly. Amid the mirth, the sorrows of our order from the past year strangle my soul. But this is the part in this improv show where I stand up and bounce back for all of us. "I will never forget my service training ground: the colony. How many of our nearest and dearest floated up the chimneys of its crematories? I dedicate my service to all of us in their memory." The silence of this assembly deafens in a way that no cacophony ever could. Yet it is a healing, holy moment of silence. Taken without request, this moment happens naturally, from our collective soul. "Thank you again," I conclude.

I return to our table, drinking up the spirit of our assembly, the brain of the body of Rodentia. My scurry catches me up to the collective will of our species. I'm quite comfortable to be a worker bee among worker bees. But please, let us all be bees and not wasps or religious spiders of self-centered arrogance.

The time comes when all in attendance may freely share before the assembly. Set up at each side of the hall, the public microphone stations wait for the rodents lining up to pose questions, give brief statements, and simply give a voice to the masses before the capstone. Comrade Cappuccino steps up to the microphone at the left.

"Greetings from the Rocky Mountains, everyone. My name is Sister Senior Medical Retriever Cappuccino, and I serve the All Rodents Evolutionary Union!"

"Greetings, Comrade Cappuccino!" the assembly responds.

"I just want to give my fellow Rocky Mountaineer, Comrade GenSec-to-be Fearless some big, big love and respect, and a whole lot of honor . . ." She weeps out of nowhere. But she bounces back through her tears and mournful peeping to finish her thought. ". . . Because Comrade Fearless is a rat worthy of his name. Fearless fits him perfectly! We met on a thorning battlefield! Then he saved me in the bug-thorning ROCOCOLACO colony!"

"Sister? Would you please keep your confession clean?" the beaver at the chairmouse's post whistles.

Cappuccino checks her spleen, but I think she could kill that beaver right now. But she finishes the tribute. "I apologize. Really, I do. But I never met a real leader like our fearless leader, Fearless. Hey! Get a load of this one. Comrade GenSec-to-be Fearless! Let me be the first to address you as 'Fearless Leader!'"

## THE END

# ACKNOWLEDGMENTS

I would like to thank the novelist Richard Fifield for all his input into this work, when it was a two hundred page manuscript, but not a story. And all of my beta readers who commented on the concept. Their input and honesty directed this work into becoming a good story, well told. And to Drea Michelle Farley, who appears in our original video trailer.

**T. William Pleasant** began creating stories for movies when he child. After so many performing arts and English credits at the University of Montana, he chose to dive into his passion for visual storytelling, bought a new computer with screenwriting software, quit his day job and went to work. Vanguard of Nature came out of the idea of a reflection of human nature. Today Mr. Pleasant lives out west, but Planet Earth is his backyard.

www.ingramcontent.com/pod-product-compliance
Lightning Source LLC
Chambersburg PA
CBHW031544260326
41914CB00002B/255